AN AGE AGO

AN AGE AGO

*A Selection of
Nineteenth-Century
Russian Poetry*

SELECTED AND
TRANSLATED BY ALAN MYERS
WITH A FOREWORD AND
BIOGRAPHICAL NOTES
BY JOSEPH BRODSKY

Farrar · Straus · Giroux
NEW YORK

Translation copyright © 1988 by
Farrar, Straus and Giroux, Inc.
Foreword and biographical notes
copyright © 1988 by Joseph Brodsky
All rights reserved
Printed in the United States of America
Published simultaneously in Canada by
Collins Publishers, Toronto
Designed by Cynthia Krupat
First edition, 1988
Library of Congress Cataloging-in-Publication Data
An age ago.
1. Russian poetry—19th century—Translations into
English.   2. English poetry—Translations from Russian.
I. Myers, Alan.
PG3237.E5A3   1988   891.71'3'08   86-22947

Contents

A. S. PUSHKIN

E. A. BARATYNSKY

Foreword

Like many a closed book, the nineteenth century has never been read through. Absorbing dust, it sits on the shelf of time, available to our scrutiny but seldom touched. This is so perhaps because whenever one bothers to peruse it one discovers its pages contain nearly every insight or concept which our century claims as its own achievement. Even if one wants to make an exception for the modern notion of speed, of qualitative acceleration, one is bound to realize that this, too, has been taken care of by that century's music; that *Star Wars* could be easily scored by any of Beethoven's piano sonata prestos.

A publisher more prudent than time, of course, would have had that century issued in several volumes, rather than squeeze Napoleon and Queen Victoria (or Shelley and Dostoevsky) under the same cover. Still, what is most interesting about this conventional edition is not so much the diversity of its contents as the way it robs us of the benefit of hindsight. The previous century staunchly refuses to become our past, both by shaming our present attention span and by forcing upon us an intensity of focus we are seldom capable of. The mode of mental conduct the nineteenth century's authors offer compromises modern reality to the point of our suspecting it as having been used in their works, as having already taken place among their pages—to the point of some grammatical *déjà vu*.

This ability—to deliver blows to our principle of causality—alone would suffice to proclaim the book of the nineteenth century closed. After all, that was precisely the century which, as it were, coined the concept of biological determinism. Besides, the sense of superiority felt by the alive and present toward the dead and absent—a sense usually conveyed by chronology—suggests, in its own right, that a century, in order to be fully comprehended, requires perhaps yet another century.

As conventions go, chronology is presumably not the worst among them and can be regarded as an attempt to structure our nostalgia for our betters, or for a better scale of reality. Today this nostalgia is most likely at its sharpest, for in our minds there still vibrate a few logical links connecting us to the nineteenth century. Tomorrow these links will be gone, missed, replaced with the sense of incongruity out of which the new world could well forge more lasting chains for its mental proletariat or bourgeoisie.

What we call the nineteenth century marks what appears to be the last period in the history of our species when its scale of reality was quantitatively human. Numerically at least, an individual's interplay with his likes was not any different from that in, say, antiquity. It was the last century of seeing, not glimpsing; of responsibility, not the incoherence of guilt. Similarly, no matter how homicidal one might have felt, one still lacked the means to commit what would pass today as mass murder. Relations with space were based on the pace of one's own step; and whenever one traveled, one did so in a charabanc driven by the same number of horses as a Roman chariot; i.e., by four or, at best, six. The invention of the engine, whose efficacy is measured in so many hundred horsepower (i.e., in such scores of these animals that there is no way to assemble and harness them for the purposes of coherent motion), chipped a lot from the reality of space and soiled what remained with abstractions hitherto confined to the works of one's imagination tackling either the life of sentiments or that of time.

That was the real, not the calendar, end of the nineteenth century. That is, its poets, up to then, could be more easily understood by their Latin counterparts than by ourselves. The acceleration of pace (subject more of enjoyment than of manly regret) has set us clearly apart, if only due to its curtailing effects on any form of commitment or concentration. For a man traveling at bullet or supersonic speed to his destination, it is difficult to comprehend wounded honor, the grid of class barriers, someone's brooding over a ruined estate, the contemplation of a single tree, or ambivalence at prayer. Yet such was the stuff of the nineteenth century's poetry, concerned with the movements of the individual soul, whose evolutions turned out to foreshadow all the laws of thermo- and aerodynamics.

To put it differently: an age ago, much less stood between man and his thoughts about himself than today. It appears he knew how to use this proximity. That is, he knew practically as much as we do about the natural and social sciences; however, he had not yet fallen victim to this knowledge. He stood, as it were, on the very threshold of that captivity, largely unaware of the impending danger; apprehensive perhaps, but free. Therefore, what he can tell us about himself, about the circumstances of his soul or mind, is of historical value in the sense that history is always free people's monologue to slaves.

A grateful and curious reader will no doubt want to learn more about the lives of those assembled within this slim volume. Sent to the right encyclopedias, monographs, dissertations, biographical notes, he, however, will not wind up with much: children of their age, Russian poets of the nineteenth century did not, with one or two exceptions, live long. Products of their class, they were not brought up to leave much of a record behind them.

A century ago, a poet's days could be shortened by, among other things, epidemics, the chains of a dungeon, a bullet received on the battlefield or in the course of a duel, a capsized boat, or a badly dressed wound. With their beloveds lost, roughly equally, to childbirth and abortion, the life expectancy of poets, even in polite society, was not terribly high. This is no doubt one way to account for the lyrical pitch of this century's poetry.

If the fates of most of this volume's contributors sound somewhat similar, it is because to be born a century ago into the Russian Empire was to be born into a fairly rigid existential pattern. Most of these writers belonged to the class of impoverished gentry—the class which is almost solely responsible for the emergence of literature everywhere. Most of them joined the Hussars or some such thing and fought either Napoleon or national minorities at the Empire's outskirts. All of them tried and failed to live by the pen. All stayed for a while in Saint Petersburg to make a splash there, and then retired to their native estates or their spouse's. Hence, perhaps, this incessant quest in Russian literature for the unique through the thick of the ordinary—the quest in the course of which both the Grail and the obstacle develop equally sacred dimensions, their shabby appearances notwithstanding. And in Russia this sensibility was voiced for the first time by Russian poets of the first quarter of the nineteenth century. This is what binds together the poems in this volume—more so even than the fates of their authors.

From the point of view of a Russian, the main

events of the nineteenth century were the Great Patriotic War of 1812, the Decembrists' rebellion of 1825, the Crimean War of 1853–56, and the Peasant Reform of 1861. To that, one may well add, the assumption of power in 1825 by Nicholas I and in 1855 by Alexander II—as well as the assassination of Alexander in 1881. Of these events, the first two left a more noticeable trace in poetry than the others —presumably because it was easier for poets of that time to identify themselves with the defense of the homeland or with republican sentiments than with the geopolitical and legislative issues of the subsequent epoch. With a few exceptions, Russian poetry of the nineteenth century appears to be introspective and personal rather than overtly topical. This is partly why, even a hundred years later, it does not speak in unison.

A good poem, in a sense, is like a photograph that puts its subjects' metaphysical features into sharp focus. Accordingly, a good poet is one who does this sort of thing in a camera-like fashion: quite unwittingly, almost in spite of himself. A poem, of course, should be memorable, yet what commits it to memory is not its linguistic texture alone. The push is given by the metaphysics, by the semblance of universal value in the statement. In the first quarter of the nineteenth century, this effect was created by a poem's tremolo; in the second, it would come in the guise of psychological observation. Russian poetry of the nineteenth century—of its first half especially—should be read if only because it gives you an idea of what gave birth to that century's Russian psychological novel.

Frequently, a certain stylistic idiom is the work of one generation. In the case of this anthology's contributors, one can argue about an entire literature being the product of one generation. Furthermore, this literature—the literature of a constellation of poets known as the Pushkin Pleiad—was also the product of singular friendships. It grew out of supper conversations, morose card games, letters, brawls, the sharing of servants, mistresses, or an opera box, as much as from the common knowledge of Greek and Latin classics, fascination with the Enlightenment and the French Revolution, worship of Lord Byron and reading of Karamzin. But, apart from all these, what the members of that Pleiad had in common were their aesthetic ideals, entertained against the most unlikely background of their country—that is, they were equally haunted by the radiance of those ideals and by the impossibility of their attainment. It is the incompatibility of those ideals with that background which earned them the label of Romantics, which fueled their absolutist attitude toward art, which enabled them to put their subjects into universal perspective, which introduced into their work a rather abstract and otherworldly tune of pure time. Indeed, incompatibilities of this sort can only be resolved through high-pitched lyricism or by way of a metronome monotone.

By the end of this volume, the reader will have come to terms with those strange-sounding un-English names and will even feel a bit suspicious of the cadence of their verses. "No doubt the translator is pulling my leg!" he will exclaim. "This is simply a stylization. The translator uses this dated diction to convey a sense of distance, of a different century."

This remark will be correct only insofar as the distance between the modern and the previous century's locution is really measurable. For, young though Russian poetry was a century ago, metrically, to say the least, it was as mature as her Western sisters. If the music of some of these poems sounds familiar, it is not because Mr. Alan Myers did not know better but because meters are meters no matter the language in which they are employed. That is what they are meters for.

In fact, one should be grateful to Mr. Myers for his consistent attempt to retain as many formal aspects of the original as possible. If, because of that, a poem in translation appears to resemble a poem written a century ago in English, so much the better. What dictates a translator's choice of this or that piece of work in a foreign language is the existence of equivalent means in his own. However, the aforementioned resemblance is unlikely to occur. And by the same token, one should not make the mistake of searching for English or American parallels to Evgeny Baratynsky, Prince Vyazemsky, Aleksandr Pushkin or Feodor Tyutchev, Mikhail Lermontov, or others. There are none; but it is not so much a sense of futility that should prevent such quests as an apprehension that thinking in parallels bypasses a lot of reality. Alien to the nature of literature, this type of analysis reduces one's sense of existential options; ultimately, it compromises time itself.

Benefit of hindsight this type of thinking has not. Looking through the little window of this anthology onto the nineteenth century, we should try to see it for what it was, for what it felt about itself. We should not apply here our new, high-resolution lenses —which lose the whole for the sharp details—for the main virtue of the nineteenth century was, precisely, its ability to keep both things steadily in focus. That is why the translator has tried to preserve as many features of the original as he could. This way, perhaps, we may see better that century's noble though somewhat shabby figure, a silhouette really, of somebody who was born at Austerlitz, who died with the steam engine and legislation, and who had us for the future.

Joseph Brodsky

January 16, 1986

V. A. Zhukovsky

{ 1 7 8 3 — 1 8 5 2 }

Friendship

Rolled down from some high mountain brow,
An oak lay on the earth, by lightning bolts
    confounded;
The supple ivy, too, so closely wrapped around it . . .
    O Friendship, such art thou!

1805

Song

The ring of my true lover
I dropped into the sea;
And with it every prospect
Of happiness for me.

When giving it she warned me:
"Just wear it from now on!
While it is on your finger
You are my only one!"

The day of my misfortune,
While rinsing out my net,
The ring slipped off my finger—
I might be looking yet!

Since then we are like strangers,
She will not turn her head!
Since then my cheerful spirits
Lie on the ocean bed!

O wind that blows from northward
Awake and lend a hand!
Pluck up the ring and roll it
To me here on the sand.

A day ago she softened:
My tears had moved her so.

With something long-forgotten
Her eyes began to glow!

She sat beside me gently,
Caressed my fingertips;
She wanted to say something,
But nothing passed her lips!

What use are your caresses!
A civil word or not?!
It's love, love, love, I long for
And that's what I've not got!

Seek out who has a mind to
Rich amber from the sea . . .
I mourn my ring unceasing
And all it means to me.

1816

Song

Enchantment of my past existence,
Why have you come to haunt me so?
Who prompts these memories' persistence,
The voiceless dreams of long ago?
My heart has heard that whispered greeting,
Familiar eyes my soul revealed,
A vision for an instant fleeting
Of what the gulf of time concealed.

The past sweet-sacred visitation,
Why press me so insistently?
Can I say *wake*! to expectation?
Can I command what's past to *be*?
Will there be fresh illumination
To beautify that faded view?
Can I clothe in imagination
The naked life that once I knew?

For that far country why keep yearning,
Where days were such as are no more?
To lands once lost there's no returning,
Nor sight of years gone long before.
One dweller in that land reposes,
Mute witness of sweet yesterday;
Along with him those days of roses
In common grave are laid away.

1818

Remembrance

Of those dear friends of ours who lived in days of yore
And whose companionship allowed us to live through
    them,
  Say not with sighs: they are no more,
  Recall with gratitude: we knew them.

1821

Night

Exhausted, the day sinks to sleep,
To waters of crimson descending,
The heavens' bright azure is ending,
Cool shadows beginning to creep;
Gentle mid silence nocturnal
Night moves on her pathway supernal,
As Hesperus wings on before
His beauteous star lit once more.

With magical veil thence depart
And down from the heavens come stealing,
With phial of oblivion and healing
Grant peace to the weary in heart.
Your coming assuages the anguish
Of souls as in torment they languish,
Your soft singing lulls the oppressed
Like mother with child, bringing rest.

1823

March 19, 1823

You stood before me
In silent sadness,
Your contemplation
Charged with emotion,
Potent reminder
Of former sweetness . . .
It was the last time
This side of heaven.

You parted from me,
A silent angel;
Your grave is peaceful
As paradise is.
There lie all earthly
Fond recollections
And all the holy
Deep thoughts of heaven.

Skies filled with stars,
Still of the night . . .

1823

K. N. Batyushkov

{ 1 7 8 7 – 1 8 5 5 }

Sunt aliquid Manes: letum non omnia finit,
Luridaque evictos effugit umbra rogos.
—PROPERTIUS

As I was leaving Albion's shore, mist-covered,
O'erwhelmed by leaden waves it seemed to sink from
     view.
  Behind the ship a halcyon still hovered
Whose quiet voice gave heart to all our sailor crew.
  The slap of waves, the ev'ning sea breeze drowsing,
The same unchanging creak and flutter of the sails,
  The cry of helmsman from the deck arousing
The watchman wave-lulled there and leaning by the
     rails—
  All things induced a mood of meditation.
I stood close by the mast, entranced and sunk in
     thought,
  And through the haze and darkness' slow invasion
The northern luminary's kindly light I sought.
  My mind became engrossed in past emotion,
The land where I was born, the sweetness of those
     skies.
  But soon the moaning wind, the rocking of the
     ocean
Induced a languorous oblivion on my eyes.
  I leaned, quite given up to dreaming,
And then—was it a dream?—he stood there in the
     night,
  My comrade who had perished in the fight,
An envied death, by Pleisse's waters streaming.
  The shade did not affright: his brow
  Preserved no trace of wounding bestial;

Like mornings fresh in May, pure gladness glowed
    there now,
And all about his face recalled a soul celestial.
" 'Tis you, then, comrade sweet, the friend of better
    days!
    'Tis you, then?" I exclaimed. "Oh, you who fell
    sublimely!
Was it not I that stood above your grave untimely,
Against the background of Bellona's fearful rays?
    Did I then, with my fellows vying,
Inscribe your noble deeds on oak trees with my sword,
Escort your shade to gain its heavenly reward
    With sobs and prayers and bitter crying?
Shade unforgettable! Make answer, brother brave!
Or were those past events but idle dream-creation:
All, all—the bloodless corpse, the ritual, the grave—
A figment friendship formed in my imagination?
Oh, say one word to me, some sound familiar lend
    Once more, my eager ear caressing,
And let this hand of mine, O unforgotten friend,
Take yours and love lie in the pressing . . ."
But as I flew to him . . . the lofty spirit fled
Into the blue abyss unclouded overhead
Like smoke, a meteor, a specter of the midnight,
    Was gone—and slumber left my sight.

All round lay fast asleep, in brooding silence lapped.
The mighty elements themselves seemed hardly
    waking.

Lit only by a moon, now dim and cloud-enwrapped,
With zephyr scarcely felt, the waves were barely
    breaking.
But, as for me, all calm had long since vanished hence.
    To overtake that ghost my soul felt driven,
Still hoping to detain my visitor from heaven—
O thou, my brother dear! O thou, the best of friends!

1814

To My Friends

Here then my list of works,
Where friends may find some part at least to treasure;
    I know, by my good angel's measure,
    That in this labyrinth of rhyme and words
    True art wins small devotion:
But friendship here will see, instead, my own
        emotion,
    The story of my passion's prime,
    Delusions of my thought and feeling;
The vanities, the cares, the grief of former time,
    The airy pleasures, lightly wheeling;
    How oft I stumbled, rose up straight,
    Or vanished from the world's attention;
How once again my skiff set out to challenge fate . . .
    My journal, so to state,
Where friendly eyes will see a poet free from tension,
    And thus will set him down:
    "Our friend was fickle in obedience;
In Paphos wayward seemed, on Pindus' slopes a
        clown;
But friendship, be it said, retained his full allegiance;
By reason of his pen, no friend was e'er the worse
    (A wonder on Parnassus, sadly);
He lived the way he wrote his verse . . .
    Not well—but not too badly!"

1817

There is enjoyment in a wilderness of trees,
    A pleasure by the salty ocean,
There is a concord in the swell of heavy seas,
    Cascading down in mindless motion.
I love my near and dear, but, Mother Nature, yet
    Within my heart you are the stronger!
With you, O sovereign one, I can at once forget
    Both what I was, when I was younger,
And what I have become beneath the chill of time.
    Through you my senses have awoken:
My soul cannot express these things in graceful
      rhyme
    Yet cannot let them stay unspoken.

1819

You've heard that saying brave,
Of old Melchizedek when he was near his grave?
That man was born to be a slave,
And dies one in due season,
And death will furnish him no reason
Why man still treads this grievous vale of tears,
And suffers, weeps, and disappears.

1821

Prince P. A. Vyazemsky

{ 1 7 9 2 – 1 8 7 8 }

The Russian God

Do you need an explanation
what the Russian God can be?
Here's a rough approximation
as the thing appears to me.

God of snowstorms, God of potholes,
every wretched road you've trod,
coach inns, cockroach haunts, and ratholes—
that's him, that's your Russian God.

God of frostbite, God of famine,
beggars, cripples by the yard,
farms with no crops to examine—
that's him, that's your Russian God.

God of breasts and . . . all sagging,
swollen legs in bast shoes shod,
curds gone curdled, faces dragging—
that's him, that's your Russian God.

God of brandy, pickle vendors,
those who pawn what serfs they've got,
of old women of both genders—
that's him, that's your Russian God.

God of medals and of millions,
God of yard sweepers unshod,

lords in sleighs with two postilions—
that's him, that's your Russian God.

Fools win grace, wise men be wary,
there he never spares the rod,
God of everything contrary—
that's him, that's your Russian God.

God of all that gets shipped in here,
unbecoming, senseless, odd,
God of mustard on your dinner—
that's him, that's your Russian God.

God of foreigners, whenever
they set foot on Russian sod,
God of Germans, now and ever—
that's him, that's your Russian God.

1828

Tears

Countless tears I've shed, yet
many more were quelled
and denied their outlet:
secret grief withheld.

Those I let flow freely
are forgotten quite;
they refreshed and healed me:
sweet dewfall at night.

Those that sank and rested
on the heart's deep floor
turned to ulcers, festered:
cancer at the core.

1829

The Tear

Whenever grief's insistent pressure
prompts storms within your soul to rise,
reluctant tears of fine displeasure
begin to well up in your eyes.

Then I am lost in delectation,
admire more tenderly, all care,
your features' gentle perturbation,
that most becoming grief you wear.

Enchanting azure eyes then mingle
with wav'ring gleam of tears, a spell
that melts me wholly; now a single
pure pearl rolls from its turquoise shell.

1829

I have outlived most things and people round me
and weighed the worth of most things in this life;
these days I drag along though bars surround me,
exist within set limits without strife.
Horizons now for me are close and dreary
and day by day draw nearer and more dark.
Reflection's dipping flight is slow and weary,
my soul's small world is desolate and stark.
My mind no longer casts ahead with boldness,
the voice of hope is dumb—and on the route,
now trampled flat by living's mundane coldness,
I am denied the chance to set my foot.
And if my life has seemed among the hardest
and though my storeroom's stock of grain is small,
what sense is there in hoping still for harvest
when snow from winter clouds begins to fall?
In furrows cropped by scythe or sickle clearance
there may be found, it's true, some living trace;
in me there may be found some past experience,
but nothing of tomorrow's time or space.
Life's balanced the accounts, she is unable
to render back what has been prised away
and what the earth, in sounding vaults of marble,
has closed off, pitiless, from light of day.

1837

Remembrance

To countries far from here, beneath an alien heaven,
Should you desire to bear a living souvenir
Of lands that gave you birth or those whom you hold
    dear,
A verse, to touch the heart at times that seem
    God-given
And, trusty sentinel, call "Russia" to the driven,
Or should misfortune come to put you to the test
Or homesickness begin to stir and gnaw the breast,
Do not expect from me some joyous affirmation;
The muse has laid aside her songs of inspiration,
The chaplet of bright roses fallen from her brow.
In mourning garments sorrowfully shrouded,
She guards the precious urn with eyes downcast and
    clouded,
Condemned to be the muse of ceaseless weeping now.
When close to foreign shores the buoyant waves have
    brought you,
When yet the sounds of home still faintly cling and
    haunt you
And sadly pierce your heart and find response
    therein,
One thought alone fills me, one sad event within:
Remembrance of the past and keepsake for tomorrow,
My valediction take, a single word of sorrow,
For such access of grief is more than I can bear;
A faithful monument to heart-deep tears and
    mourning,

My weeping voice repeats to all those over there:
The brightest star we had has fallen without warning,
Is suddenly plucked down amid the tempest's rage,
The purest of the songs of our poetic age
Is suddenly struck dumb, the lyre leaves off its story;
Our laurels in their prime, the very flush of glory,
Now fall, our vatic bays, our epoch's sweet delight,
That with their rustling stems and sweet melodious
      singing
Have roused prophetic boughs from slumber's deepest
      night,
Sent forth the tongue of gods across the grim North
      winging;
Forever silent now, the poet we adore,
And we are steeped in grief, for Pushkin is no more.

1837

To Natalia Nikolaevna Pushkina

In memory of me, when I am long departed,
write in your notebook: here he was a loyal friend
and *there* his prayers will mention me; though parted,
there, too, he will be mine.

      And you, when duties lend
a furtive hour to pass alone and meditating,
on these few sheets of paper, fresh and crisply white,
note all down freely in your flowing hand, dictating
a true confession of your thoughts by day and night,
those errors willed by you and those by chance
  committed,
hopes dashed and tears and smiles, let nothing be
  omitted,
the secret flaring of the banked fires of the heart,
which all unwillingly your flushing cheeks betoken;
your day inscribe within, a living work of art,
with all that's said to you and what remains unspoken,
but which the eye shows forth, though words are not
  expressed
and all that in yourself is secretly repressed.
Above all, be sincere—bad faith brings retribution.
But your each word, each inner feeling, speaks aright
and in advance you gain from me your absolution,
  your chaplain and your acolyte.

1841

A. S. Pushkin

{ 1 7 9 9 – 1 8 3 7 }

To Chaadaev

Our dreams of love and modest glory,
delusive hopes now quickly sped,
our pranks and games, our youth's brief story
like sleep or morning mist are fled;
and yet, within, desires still quicken,
our souls impatient for their hour,
while yoked beneath a fateful power
our country calls to us, heart-stricken.
We wait now, wearied-out with yearning
lest sacred freedom come too late,
as some young lover, too, might wait
the tryst for which his heart is burning.
So while for freedom's flame we live
and honor in our breast we treasure,
friend, let us to our homeland give
the noblest that our souls can measure.
My comrade, trust: she will yet rise
that star of captivating splendor,
the sleep will leave our country's eyes
and on the shards of tsardom's grandeur
our two names will be incised.

1818

K * * *

That wondrous instant of our meeting—
my mind's eye sees you standing there,
a vision transient and fleeting,
true beauty's spirit, pure and rare.

In toils of hopeless grief confounded,
amid life's noise and stress it seems
for long that tender voice resounded
and those sweet features came in dreams.

Years passed; the storms that life engenders
dispersed my former hopes of grace
and I forgot those accents tender,
the heavenly beauty of your face.

And in my dark incarceration
my days passed like the clouds above,
bereft alike of inspiration,
of tears, of life itself, of love.

My soul awoke to new existence,
again you stood before me there,
a vision lasting but an instant,
true beauty's spirit, pure and rare.

My heart relives the old sensation
and once more steal down from above,

God's benediction, inspiration,
and tears, and life itself and love.

1825

To Vyazemsky

It seems the sea, that scourge of ages,
Contrives your genius to inspire?
You laud upon your golden lyre
Old Neptune's trident as he rages.

Don't waste your praise. These days you'll find
That sea and land have no division.
On any element mankind
Is tyrant, traitor, or in prison.

1826

Arion

A goodly number shipped as crew;
some helped to set the sail and trim it,
while others, straining to the limit,
dug deep the oars. In silence, too,
our trusty helmsman checked our motion
and, wordless, steered our weighty craft;
while I, still carefree, sang and laughed
to cheer the oars . . . Then fore and aft
a roaring tempest ripped the ocean,
engulfing helmsman, mast, and yard!—
But I, the enigmatic bard,
was saved and cast up on the shoreline,
and tune my lyre with skillful stroke,
while drying off my sodden cloak
beneath the rocks here in the sunshine.

1827

Message to Siberia

In deep Siberian mines retain
A proud and patient resignation;
Your grievous toil is not in vain
Nor yet your thought's high aspiration.

Grief's constant sister, hope is nigh,
Shines out in dungeons black and dreary
To cheer the weak, revive the weary;
The hour will come for which you sigh,

When love and friendship reaching through
Will penetrate the bars of anguish,
The convict warrens where you languish,
As my free voice now reaches you.

Each hateful manacle and chain
Will fall; your dungeons break asunder;
Outside waits freedom's joyous wonder
As comrades give you swords again.

1827

The Prophet

Athirst for spiritual good,
I dragged my steps through wastelands **weary**,
Until a six-winged seraph stood
Before me on a crossroads dreary;
He touched my eyes, or so it seemed,
With fingers light as if I dreamed:
Now armed with a prophetic power
They opened wide like birds that cower.
His touch then lighted on my ears,
Which filled with music of the spheres;
I heard the heavens' subtle shaking,
The flight of angels up above,
The tread of sea beasts as they move,
The life in valley vineyards waking.
And now toward my lips he bent,
From whence my sinful tongue he rent,
With all its slanders, idly blurted,
And now a wise old serpent's sting
Into my mouth, a nerveless thing,
His skilled and bloody hand inserted.
Then with a sword my breast he split,
Drew out my very heart, still racing,
A blazing coal instead of it
Within my gaping chest then placing.
As corpse-like on the sand I lay,
The voice of God I heard to say,
"Arise, O prophet, watch and listen,
To execute my will and plan,

Cross land and sea, fulfill your mission,
With words ignite the heart of man!"

1828

When wand'ring along noisy alleys
or standing in some crowded shrine,
with youngsters and their witless sallies,
I drift into these dreams of mine.

My thoughts run thus: the years are speeding,
however many may be here,
to vaults eternal all are heading
and someone's hour is always near.

I contemplate a lonely holm oak,
think to myself: That monarch sage
will long outlive my paltry epoch
as he outlived my father's age.

Should I but hold an infant tender,
my mind's eye sees the parting day!
To you I yield, my place surrender:
for you the bloom, for me decay.

Every season, each day's dawning
I follow with anxiety,
attempting to predict the morning
my coming death will choose for me.

And where will Fate pounce as I wander?
In battle, traveling, at sea?

Or will that valley over yonder
ere long receive the last of me?

And though my cold and senseless carcass
may rot as well below, above,
yet I would wish to meet the darkness
close by the place I know and love.

And even at the graveyard's entrance
fresh-springing life will sport and play
and nature in sublime indifference
will shine on in undying day.

1829

The Georgian hills above lie shrouded in the night;
    Aragva churns down in the hollow,
I feel both sad and gay, my grief suffused with light;
    Your presence permeates my sorrow,
Just you and you alone . . . My melancholy fit
    Is undisturbed, no outside thing to bother,
My heart once more is warmed to love, and it
    Must love, for it can do no other.

1829

. . .

I loved you once: of love, perhaps, an ember
Within my soul is not extinguished yet;
But let that be no prompting to remember,
Or be a cause of sadness or regret.
I loved you once, quite hopeless, dumbly tender,
By jealousy and diffidence oppressed;
I loved you once with such complete surrender
As may God grant you may again be blessed.

1829

To a Poet

No poet should set store by public acclamation.
Ecstatic praise will pass, an instant in the ear;
The empty crowd will laugh, the fool have his oration,
But you must stay quite calm, unbending, and
    austere.

A king, then, live alone. You choose your destination,
Go where your questing mind shall now elect to steer
To bring perfection to the thoughts you hold most
    dear,
Requiring no rewards, achieving consummation—

They lie within yourself. As judge you are the best;
In valuing your works, severer than the rest,
Do they bring you delight, O artist most exacting?

They please you? Well, then, let the crowd protest
And spit upon the shrine where burns your fire
    blessed,
And rock your tripod in their childish, rough
    play-acting.

1830

. . .

For God's sake, let me not go mad;
far better beggar's staff and plaid,
    and toil or hunger choose.
But not that I would grimly cling
to intellect as to a thing
    I greatly fear to lose:

Were I but left at liberty
to roam at will, exultantly
    I'd race by woods and streams!
And sing delirious, overjoyed,
oblivious in a swirling void
    of wild and wondrous dreams.

Enrapt in dreams that never cloy,
I'd gaze aloft, suffused with joy,
    into the empty skies;
I would be willful, wild, and free,
a whirlwind roaring from the sea,
    destroying as it flies.

But there's the rub: once lose your mind
and you're a terror to mankind;
    they'll take you when they please,
attach you to the idiot's chain
and through the bars time and again
    they'll come to poke and tease.

At night the sounds that I shall hear
will not be nightingales, I fear;
    no oak woods' solemn strains
but cries of those who share my plight,
the curse of warders in the night,
    and shrieks and clank of chains.

1833

It's time, my dear, it's time! The heart demands its
    quittance—
As day flies after day and each bears off its pittance
Withdrawn from living's store and meanwhile you
    and I
Draw up our plans to live . . . And then—why, then,
    we'll die.
No happiness exists, but there is calm and freedom;
And long an enviable fate I've dreamed on—
And long, a worn-out slave, I've contemplated flight
To some far-off abode of art and pure delight.

1834

Elegy

Extinguished are my years of carefree laughter;
They weigh me down, a heavy morning after.
But, just like wine, the grief I must assuage
Within my soul grows stronger now with age.
My road is grim. My future sea is stormy
And promises but grief and toil before me.

But, O my friends, I have no wish to sink;
I burn to live, to suffer, and to think;
I know there will be joy and delectation
Among the griefs, the cares and agitation,
The ecstasy of harmony be mine,
My fancy draw sweet tears from me like wine,
And it may be—upon my sad declining
True love will smile, a valediction shining.

1834

. . .

        . . . I visit once again
this little plot of earth where once I spent
in exile two whole years that passed unnoticed.
A good ten years have gone since then—and many
are the alterations in my life,
and I, obedient to the general ruling,
have undergone some change—but here again
what's past and gone still threatens to engulf me;
I wandered only yesterday, it seems,
about these woodlands.

              Here's the little homestead
where my poor nanny lived along with me.
She's gone now long ago—upon the staircase
I'll hear no more the heavy sound of footsteps,
the scrupulous patrol she mounted on me.
The wooded hillside—up above there, often
I used to sit unmoving and gaze down
upon the lake, beset with glum reflections
recalling other shores and other wavelets . . .
Between the golden cornfields and green pastures
the lake itself spreads wider, ever bluer;
and on the breast of unplumbed depths of water
the fisher floats and drags along behind
his tattered trawl net. By the shores, steep-sloping,
the villages lie scattered—while beyond them
a crooked windmill leans, just barely turning
its sail-arms in the zephyr . . .

On the border
of Granddad's broad estate, on that same spot
whereat the road goes climbing up the hillside,
scoured bare around by rainfall, three pines grow—
one standing at a distance, while two others
take closer order—here, when oft I passed them
while mounted on my horse out in the moonlight,
with friendly sound of rustling in their tops
they ever greeted me. Along that pathway
I just now rode and there before me
I saw them once again. They stood as always,
that selfsame breeze and so-familiar rustle—
but round about their roots, now gnarled and knotted
(where once upon a time the earth lay naked),
a youthful grove of saplings had grown up,
a family of green; the bushes clustered
beneath their shade like children. While far off
there stood alone their gloomy old companion
like some stout bachelor, and round his bole,
as formerly, grew nothing.
                    Greetings, O tribe,
so young and unbeknown to me! Not I
shall ever see your mighty final soaring,
when you shall have outgrown my old familiars
and stand between and shield their ancient heads
from eyes of travelers. My grandson, though,
will hearken to your murmuring when he,

returning late from friends and conversation
and filled with gay and pleasant speculation,
will pass close by you in the gloom of nightfall
and suddenly recall me.

1835

E. A. Baratynsky

{ 1 8 0 0 – 1 8 4 4 }

Disillusion

I pray you, do not idly tempt me,
rekindling passion's former blaze;
one now disillusioned, empty,
is deaf to wiles of former days.
I have no faith in protestations,
I have no faith in love at all,
no more can I accept her thrall,
her treacherous hallucinations!
Do not provide fresh cause to weep;
of former bliss, I pray, no murmur,
and, friend solicitous, show firmer
purpose in permitting me to sleep!
I drowse, and slumber sweetly takes me;
forget those dreams of yesteryear;
for now great agitation shakes me,
but that, not love, is all you stir.

1821

My gift is scant, my voice lacks force behind it,
and yet I live and my existence here
to somebody perhaps is counted dear:
some far descendant possibly may find it
within my verse: who knows? Our souls far-flung
will thus turn out to have some close relation,
and as I found a friend this generation,
a reader shall I find in time to come.

1828

Death

I will not call Death darkness' daughter
nor, slave to some received idea,
equip her with the tools of slaughter
as graveyard skeletons appear.

O daughter of the realms supernal!
O radiant beauty's rarest shade!
Your hands bear olive, peace eternal,
no scything, all-destroying blade.

When out this flow'ring world came leaping
from savage forces' equal strife,
Almighty God into your keeping
consigned its working and its life.

And you fly up above creation,
dispensing concord's influence,
and with your cooling inspiration
you calm mere being's turbulence.

You curb betimes the mad commotion
of hurricanes' o'erpow'ring roar
as you turn back the raging ocean
when oft it dashes to the shore.

And you set bounds to vegetation
so that no giant woods may rise

to threaten earth's obliteration,
or grass grow upwards to the skies.

And, as for man, by all that's holy!
At your approach his cheeks turn white;
high-colored wrath at once ebbs wholly—
lascivious flushes vanish quite.

Your impartial law redresses
the wrongs of man's unequal fate:
that selfsame hand of yours caresses
both serving wretch and potentate.

This mixed oppression and confusion,
the age we live in and its pains—
all problems find their resolution
in you, dissolver of all chains.

1828

The Muse

I am not dazzled by my muse's features,
for her the name of beauty is too grand;
young men do not at once become her creatures
or languish after her, a lovesick band.
The latest style is not her affectation,
nor flashing eyes, nor sparkling conversation,
with suchlike artifice she has no truck,
and yet the world at times is somewhat struck
by something in her face beyond the common,
a calm simplicity of word or phrase,
so they refrain from passing wounding comment
and honor her instead with idle praise.

1829

Desolation

Seductive canopy, this visit I have paid,
not in the cheerful days of sweet vivacious Maytime,
when your green branches complement the daytime
and lure the passer-by into your grateful shade,
    when you exude that scent benumbing—
distilled most artfully from all your cherished
        flowers—
    into your dark enchanted bowers
    I still delayed my tardy coming.
In autumn now the trees stood naked, branch and
        root,
    aloof and silent, black negation;
the frozen blades of grass crunched soft beneath my
        foot,
the dead leaves rustled in a sudden agitation;
    through frosty coolness then I caught,
    full-on, the reek of leaves decaying;
but springtime's pristine garb was not the thing I
        sought,
    my thoughts to former years were straying.
With soul preoccupied thus, pensively I strolled
those paths well known to me from youthful years
        long vanished,
laid out by cunning hands, some artist skilled of old—
his craft, alas, by time eroded now and banished.
The paths were barely traced, as if some other, once,
had wandered here. At last I found the vale I
        cherished,

dear vale, which my first dim and halting thoughts
    had nourished,
and sought the gracious waters of the well-known
    ponds,
sought out the once-familiar surge of water leaping;
   once there, I thought, my soul will be
soon overwhelmed with crowding visions dear to
    me . . .
Great God! The stout-built dam had broken down
    and, seeping,
  its waters wandered far and wide,
  its bed now covered up in couch grass,
where sets of beehives squatted side by side;
the lightly marked-out paths now petered out in
    impasse.
In nothing could my eye descry the known!
But here the way led on across a wooded hillside
and boldly drew me forth, then suddenly . . . was
    gone,
  a landslip swallowed it . . . Alone
I stood and measured out the depth and, gloomy-eyed,
in some bewilderment sought out another route.
  I walked on: where the arbor rotted—
and in the dust before it lay its columns mute,
  the framework of a bridge still tottered.
  And you, O queen of grottoes all,
though built of heavy stone, now touched with ruin's
    finger,

seeming to crumble as I linger,
were once, in summer heat, a cool and ample hall.
What, then? Let past things fade, a fleeting summer
hour,
you are still beautiful to me, Elysian field;
though choked, your charm still holds its power,
compels my willing soul to yield.
He could not have been cold of heart or understanding
who, exquisite delights commanding,
gave all these winding paths their own peculiar bent,
who lent a ready ear to the mysterious keening
of maples, these old oaks, and, knowing what it meant,
preserved an empathy, a leaning.
For long, concerning him no rumor reached my ear,
Some far-off grave no doubt contained a rich
possession,
My mem'ry had preserved no picture, no impression,
And yet his spirit lives, still palpable, still here;
A friend to reverie and nature,
I sense him fully deep within;
He inspires my soul in ecstasy to sing,
He bids me hymn the woods, the streams, and every
creature;
He firmly gives his word that there will be a land
Where one day I shall find a springtime without end,
Where no trace of decay exists for me to see there,
And where the shady oaks, forever fresh and green,

By never-failing waters lean,
That shade most dear to me will be there.

1834

The Wineglass

Charged with liquid effervescence,
how you hiss, my sparkling wine!
Wreathed now in a misted essence,
ice-cold crystal, wineglass mine . . .
No company, no noisy drinker,
orgiasts to greet you, none;
a voluptuous freethinker,
here I sit and drink alone.

What my soul is ever rich in,
all is yours, O friend champagne!
Now my thoughts fear no restriction,
all my dreams are off the rein;
at your font of inspiration
your disciple is immune
to the petty animation
of the crowd's discordant tune.

My high mood, though injudicious,
cannot prompt the least offense;
nor, a prey to friendship specious,
blurt my inner joy intense;
nor embarrass jealous weak-wits,
ignorant and solemn fops,
by outpouring my proud secrets
or my holiest of hopes!

So, with me hold conversation,
my capricious sparkling rill!
Advocate inebriation,
life's slow poison, what you will;
legends sweet that make the heart sing
graciously revive for me,
or some long-forgotten suff'ring
call back to my memory!

O my wineglass of seclusion!
You do not make more intense
living's vulgar disillusion
like some magnifying lens;
fertile, noble, spring eternal,
you have power to bring to birth
visions straight from realms infernal,
or send dreams from heav'n to earth.

Henceforth I drink in isolation!
No seer can find celestial light
amid the world's reverberation,
desert air improves the sight!
Not vainly seeking keen sensation,
passions of the social scene,
but in lone intoxication—
light breaks through where none has been!

1835

Autumn

I

September's here; delaying his first beams,
The sun's pale light but coldly glimmers;
His rays are mirrored now in rippling streams,
Uncertain, shifting golden shimmers.
Gray mist entwines about the high hills' brow,
While dews descend to drown the level;
The leaves of tousled oaks are saffron now,
The aspen's ovals all disheveled;
Silent are the songbirds' cheerful cries
And woods lie mute beneath the soundless skies.

II

September's here; the year's nocturnal time
Draws on. Across the fields in warning,
The frost has flung by now its skein of rime,
Its silver patterns star the morning.
Cool gales will shortly herald sleet and hail;
Light clouds of dust will swirl before them,
The swaying grove will moan and rock, the vale
Will vanish under dead leaves falling;
Clouds will race across the angry sky
And darkling rivers foam as they roar by.

III

Farewell, farewell, ye burnished summer skies!
Farewell, ye tints of nature's making!
The forest filled with mystic whispering sighs,

The golden scales of water breaking!
Those happy fleeting dreams of June delight!
Echoes in the now denuded treescapes
Are mingled with the ax's ringing bite,
And soon, all powdered o'er with snowflakes,
The winter garb of forest oak and hill
Will dimly gleam in lake and frozen rill.

IV

Meanwhile, the village folk enjoy their ease
And gather in the harvest with their neighbors,
Erecting stooks of grain shorn from the leas,
And then with sickles hasten to their labors.
The sickles move as one, each finished swath
Is dotted now with sunlit haycocks;
Yet more hay lies on farm carts by the path,
Which groan beneath the weight of feedstocks;
A gold-roofed hayrick city starts to rise
And dwarfs the very peasant huts in size.

V

These days of pious rural ritual!
The smoking oven's cheerful reeking,
The thrash of flail, the grating millstone's snarl,
Aloft, the windmill's sails go creaking.
Set on, then, winter! Harsh days yet to come
Are rendered by this plowman's prudence meeker!
A joyous warmth irradiates each home

With bread and salt and foaming beaker;
With loved ones he will eat what he has grown,
The blessed fruit of labors all his own!

VI

And you, when in the autumn of your days,
O plowman of the fields of living,
And your own harvest lies before your gaze,
Your earthly sum, the gain, the giving;
And when it seems that life's deep-furrowed soil
Will now reward the toil of being,
Prepared at last to render up the spoil
Of grain sown in your youth, far-seeing,
And you begin to reap what you have wrought
And gather in your golden sheaves of thought—

VII

Can you, then, like the farmer, count your hoard?
You had, like him, a hopeful sowing;
And you, like him, once dreamed of far reward
And cherished visions golden, glowing . . .
Admire them, then! Be proud, you have them all!
Now reckon up your acquisition . . .
Alas, the dreams, the passions that enthrall,
Evoke but scorn and cold derision—
Within your soul an all-pervading shame
For all the world's deceptions and its blame.

VIII

Your day has dawned and clarity shows this—
How prone youth is to self-delusion;
For you have lived and traversed the abyss
Of human lying and confusion.
The devotee of all the pleasures once,
The burning seeker of sensation,
The king of misty splendors—seek response
From barren wastes of contemplation,
Alone at last with boredom's fell caress
Which all your haughty pride can scarce suppress!

IX

But if, by chance, a cry of rage and pain,
Some howl of anguish past restraining,
Were suddenly to well up in your brain
With wild solemnity complaining—
Then, stricken to the bone while at their sport,
Light-minded youths would halt and shiver,
The infant at his play at once stop short,
Let fall his toys and, lips a-quiver,
Leave off his joyous laughter on the spot;
The man within would die there in the cot.

X

Invite the world to celebrate and eat;
Make haste to order wines and pour them,

Then fawn and hand your guests into their seat;
Ingenious dishes set before them.
To eatables he trusts for all his fame,
All strewn about in rich profusion—
See how he glows! . . . They all taste just the same
And prompt but terror and confusion.
Then sit and hold a solitary wake
For all the worldly joys your soul can take!

XI

Whatever else henceforth within your heart
May seem like sudden comprehension,
Whatever thoughts and feelings form a part
Of that last whirlwind's great declension—
Permit the mind, in jeering triumph bold,
To quell the heart's unceasing clamor,
To quieten the vain complaints of old,
Subdue its long-belated stammer;
While you accept that crown of living's art,
Experience, the cold that numbs the heart.

XII

Or, breaking from all earthly visions free
With surges of life-giving sorrow,
The limits of the world you plainly see,
The flowering shore beyond tomorrow,
That land of condign punishment; in dreams
You trust now with renewed elation,

And orchestrating life's unruly themes
In hymns of reconciliation,
You hearken, as to harps, whose lofty strain
Was ever something foreign to your brain.

XIII

'Fore Providence, now justified, you fall
And, wholly humbled, make submission,
With hope that knows no boundaries at all
And reason that makes full admission—
Know, deep within, henceforward you will give
No heed to all the varied sounds of earth,
To trivia, those frenzied shifts to live—
Your soul's concerned with things of greater worth;
Know, rough or smooth, the life that you live through
Is not, on earth, for earth assigned to you.

XIV

As savagely sweeps down a sudden storm
And forests roar like wounded creatures,
And oceans boil as rollers swell and form
And maddened breakers smash the beaches,
It happens that the mob's light mind is caught
And roused from indolent negation
By vulgar voices peddling common thought
Among an avid congregation;
But words are held to be of little worth
When from the tongue of one who spurns the earth.

XV

Suppose, embarked upon erroneous flight
And finding no way to recover,
A heavenly star went sliding out of sight
And one star then replaced another;
The earth is not aware of it at all;
No ear on earth is turned, or traces
The plaintive distant howling of its fall,
Just as in ethereal spaces
The heavens are deaf to the ecstatic cries
That greet her newborn sister in the skies.

XVI

So winter comes, and all the starveling plain,
The spreading bald-patches of weakness,
The glowing squares of gladsome fields of grain,
The cornstalks ripening to sleekness,
Both life and death, both beggary and wealth—
Each picture of the year that's over
At one under the snow's all-shrouding stealth
'Neath one monotonous white cover—
Such is the world that henceforth you will see;
For you, alas, no harvest shall there be!

1836–37

All things have their own pace and mode of motion.
'Twixt cradle and the grave Moscow's asleep,
but even she, half deaf, hears rumors creep
that whist's old hat and a much jollier notion
is salon groups where minds have scope to soar,
where conversation reigns, and whist's a bore.
So she pursues the craze she's set her heart on—
imagine the occurrence untoward!
Salons there are, some like a kindergarten,
and some, alas, a geriatric ward.

1840

Planting a Wood

Once more it's spring; the meadows laugh once more,
the woods are gay with youthful decoration,
the villagers their tireless plows now draw
across the fields in humble aspiration.

Yet in my soul no springtime comes to bless,
nor in my soul does hope dwell undivided.
This earthly world impinges less and less,
before eternal day I close my eyelids.

The winter that now silvers my old head
keeps warm the seed from which new worlds come
      stealing;
but this bard has not passed earth's threshold yet—
to all her sons his lyre is yet appealing.

Almighty God is merciful, though just:
each moment on this earth is charged with meaning;
He will forgive the heedless prank or jest,
but never evil at its lewd convening.

If one was injured by my vaulting soul,
then he could claim from me a quittance gory;
beneath my feet instead a hidden hole
he dug and crowned his horns with fallen glory!

My soul flew out to all new tribes of men,
trained up and fostered their yet barren notions;

I gave my days to rouse them with my pen
and sang to them in praise of true emotions.

Response came none! I put aside my strings,
some other grist will prove for me more fertile!
And so to it my tender hand now brings
these tiny plants of pine, holm oak, and myrtle.

So let it be! Abandoning my songs,
I trust in this; now these shall fill their station,
from poetry, its secret griefs and wrongs,
a new-grown massive, somber generation.

1843

N. M. Yazykov

{ 1 8 0 3 – 1 8 4 6 }

Elegy

O money, money, tell me why
My purse and you are so soon parted.
For now that Christmastime is nigh,
And all good Christians glad-hearted,
I am alone, cut off from all
The promises, the expectation;
My dreams are dreams of desperation,
My finances—very small!
Oh, there, where Peter's city rises,
I'd gladly fly; 'tis dear to me,
For there the first few modest prizes
My ardent muse bestowed on me;
It can't be done, no use repining!
Sans money—what makes people glad—
No travel order for the signing
And no post-horses to be had.

A warrior on a field of woe
Might curse his fate in some such fashion
When, shattered by the stubborn foe,
He casts his spear aside in passion:
The garland not for him to wear,
No warrior's fame in saga knowing;
He looks far off—his warlike stare
Now glinting as the tears start flowing.

1823

Song

Pour one for me, friend good and true,
I am a student just like you;
I drink good wine with ne'er a fumble,
Firm vows to Bacchus I declare
And roam the world without a care,
With joy-inebriated stumble.

True freedom, cheery songs, and wine—
Enjoy them all as gifts divine,
They form a trinity most holy!
And love—well, what of love? 'Tis aye
Too cold if Bacchus be not nigh,
But with him—something too unruly!

Last night in Paradise I lay,
Both it—and she—are gone today:
She plays the role of double-dealer;
I am no slave to envy him,
Just fill my glass up to the brim:
But not to pledge thy health, O Lila!

But as for Bacchus, O my friends,
How sweet our life when he attends,
No here-today-and-gone-tomorrow:
Today, the next day, he is ours!
The joyous clink of glass o'erpowers
And drowns for aye the voice of sorrow.

1823

Elegy

Proud freedom's noble inspiration,
Since all are deaf to her command,
Stays mute, and sacred indignation
Against the Tsar lifts not her hand.

Before the despot's power infernal,
All hearts are now inured to grief,
Obedient in their yoke eternal,
While mind in mind has no belief.

I saw a Russia base and crawling,
Before the sacred altar there,
In chains, adore a sprite appalling—
'Twas for the Tsar she offered prayer!

1824

Thanksgiving

Hear my voice in glad thanksgiving!
Forswearing love, I now am free;
The desolate expanse of living
Has better paths on which to be:
Forsaking worldly tongues and duty,
I have these quiet dreams of mine,
And worship not at beauty's shrine
And am not taken in by beauty!

1824

Elegy

The people's wrath finds no expression,
The Russian mind is still in chains,
And freedom yoked in stern oppression
Conceals the thoughts of daring brains.
Those age-old bonds will never slacken
Around our homeland's patient woe:
Whole centuries will grimly flow—
Before our Russia starts to waken!

1824

M. Y. Lermontov

{ 1 8 1 4 – 1 8 4 1 }

The Sail

A white sail gleams alone out yonder
Amid the ocean's pale-blue haze . . .
What quest has driven him to wander?
Why has he left his native bays?

The waves crest as the fresh wind rises,
The mainmast bending in the breeze . . .
It is not happiness he prizes,
Nor is it happiness he flees!

Beneath, the azure current flowing;
Above, the golden sunlight glows . . .
Perverse, he seeks the storm winds blowing,
As if in storms to find repose!

1832

No, I'm not Byron, it's my role
To be an undiscovered wonder,
Like him, a persecuted wand'rer,
But furnished with a Russian soul.
I started sooner, sooner ending,
My mind will never reach so high;
Within my soul, beyond the mending,
My shattered aspirations lie:
Dark ocean answer me, can any
Plumb all your depth with skillful trawl?
Who will explain me to the many?
I . . . perhaps God? . . . No one at all?

1832

Meditation

With sadness I survey our present generation!
Their future seems so empty, dark, and cold,
Weighed down beneath a load of knowing hesitation,
In idleness stagnating, growing old.
We have received, when barely finished weaning,
The errors of our sires, their tardiness of mind,
And life oppresses us, a flat road without meaning,
    An alien feast where we have dined.
T'ward good and evil shamefully uncaring
We wilt without a fight when starting on life's race;
When danger threatens us—ignoble want of daring,
Before those set on high—despicable and base.

    A wizened fruit grown ripe before its hour,
No pleasure to the eye and no delight to taste,
An orphan stranger there, he hangs beside the
       flower—
The time of its full bloom is his to fall and waste.

For we have dried our brains with fruitless
       speculations,
Withholding enviously from friends and those about
The ringing voice of lofty aspirations
    And noble passions, undermined by doubt.
Our lips have barely brushed the cup of delectation,
    But youthful strength we did not thus retain;
From every joy we found, in fear of saturation,
    We took the best and never came again.

The dreams of poesy, pure art, and its creation
With its sweet ecstasy our senses never move;
We greedily retain the remnants of sensation—
Dug deep and miserly, a useless treasure trove.
And we both love and hate by chance, without
      conviction,
We make no sacrifice for malice, or for good,
There reigns within our souls a kind of chill
      constriction,
   Whene'er the flame ignites the blood.
The pastimes of our sires we think a boring story,
Their guileless, boyish dissipations unrefined;
We hurry to our graves, unhappy, without glory,
With one last sneering glance behind.

A gloomy throng are we, condemned and soon
      forgotten,
We pass across the world in silence, without trace,
No thoughts that might bear fruit for ages unbegotten,
   No work of genius to inspire the race.
Our ashes will receive a harsh and just portrayal,
Posterity will sneer with skilled and scornful verse,
A curse of bitterness from sons at their betrayal
   By their own father's spendthrift purse.

1838

Prayer

At life's most testing moment, when
the grieving heart's replete,
a prayer that is most potent then
I call up and repeat.

There is a power, suffused with grace,
when living words combine,
a breath beyond the commonplace,
that holds a joy divine.

Like dead-weight slipping from the brain
now fades my unbelief—
I trust again, shed tears again,
and such relief, relief . . .

1839

Testament

I feel I'd like to be alone
with you, friend, if you'll stay:
my time on earth is nearly gone;
at least that's what they say.
And you'll be going home on leave:
mind you . . . what odds? I do believe,
to tell the truth, not many
will give a brass halfpenny.

If anyone should ask of you . . .
well, anyone at all . . .
you tell them where that bullet flew
right through the chest, one ball:
"He died with honor for the Tsar"
—and say how bad our surgeons are—
"and to his habitation
he sent his salutation."

You'll likely find that my old dad
and mother both are dead . . .
I wouldn't want to make them sad
or send them tears to shed;
but if you find that they're all right,
just say I haven't time to write,
the regiment's campaigning
and there's no use complaining.

They've got a woman neighbor there . . .
God knows how long ago
we parted! . . . She will hardly care
to ask you . . . Let it go,
tell her the truth, leave out no part,
no need to spare an empty heart;
she'll shed a tear or two there . . .
but it means nothing to her!

1840

The boredom, the sadness, and no one to take by the
    hand
    Whenever your soul may be riven . . .
Ambition! . . . What use is a pointless eternal demand?
    And the years go on passing, the best you are given!
To love . . . well, but whom, then? . . . A short fling is
    not worth the chase,
    And who goes on loving forever? . . .
Perfecting the self, then? —The past has left barely a
    trace,
    The joys and the griefs—no value whatever . . .
And passion? —Well, sooner or later that sickness so
    sweet
    Is cured when you come to your senses;
And life, if you coldly assess everything that you
    meet—
    An empty and farcical set of pretenses.

1840

Gratitude

For all, O Lord, my glad thanksgiving this is:
For passion's torments suffered without end,
For bitter tears, the poison taint of kisses,
For spite of foe and calumny of friend;
For ardent spirits idly dissipated,
For all that cheated me throughout my days . . .
Grant only that I am not obligated
Much longer to express my grateful praise.

1840

Native Land

I love my native land with such perverse affection!
My better judgment has no standing here.
   Not glory, won in bloody action,
nor yet that calm demeanor, trusting and austere,
nor yet age-hallowed rites or handed-down traditions;
not one can stir my soul to gratifying visions.

   And yet I love—a mystery to me—
   her dreary steppelands wrapped in icy silence,
   her boundless, swaying, forest-mantled highlands,
   the flood waters in springtime, ample as the sea;
I love to jolt along a narrow country byway
and, slowly peering through the darkness up ahead
while sighing for a lodging, glimpse across the
      highway
the mournful trembling fires of villages outspread.
   I love the smoke of stubble blazing,
   heaped wagons on the steppe at night,
   a hill mid yellow cornfields raising,
   a pair of birch trees silver-bright.
   With pleasure few have yet discovered,
   a laden granary I see,
   a hut with straw thatch neatly covered,
   carved window shutters swinging free.
   On feast nights with the dew descending,
   I'll watch till midnight, never fear

the dance, the stamps and whistles blending
with mumbling rustics full of beer.

1841

. . .

I

I walk out alone into the darkness.
Through the mist the roadway flints gleam bright;
All is still, God speaks, the desert hearkens,
Star with star holds converse in the night.

II

Skies above show forth a solemn wonder;
Pale blue radiance laps the sleeping earth . . .
Why must I be anguished, torn asunder—
Old regrets? Or expectation's birth?

III

No, of life I have no expectation,
No regretful memories to keep,
What I seek is peace, a liberation;
I wish for oblivion, to sleep . . .

IV

Not that sleep of graveyards, chill and gruesome:
Rather for eternity to keep
Life's full powers still dormant in my bosom,
Breast still gently heaving as I sleep;

V

Have by night and day, my ear beguiling,
Voices sing sweet melodies of love,

Shady oak trees ever green and smiling
Bend their boughs and rustle close above.

1841

The Dream

A vale in Dagestan, the noon sun gleaming,
There, bullet-stricken, motionless I lay;
My wound was deep and had not ceased its steaming
As drop by drop my life blood oozed away.

I lay alone there in the sandy hollow;
The cliffs rose sharply, shelving all around,
The sun burned down on hilltops bare and yellow,
And on me, too: my sleep was deathly sound.

I dreamed a scene of lights and glowing dresses,
An evening feast back home I seemed to see;
And youthful wives with flowers in their tresses
Held cheerful conversation about me.

But taking no part in this scene of gladness,
A certain one sat thoughtful and apart;
Her soul had conjured up a scene of sadness
And, God knows how, it had possessed her heart.

A vale in Dagestan came in her dreaming,
A well-known body in that valley lay;
The body bore a chest wound black and steaming
And blood ran down and, cooling, ebbed away.

1841

Farewell to Russia's unwashed features,
To lords above, to slaves below,
And you who wear the sky-blue breeches
And you the plebs who love them so.

The mountain walls of far Caucasia
May hide me from your fell viziers,
From their cold eyes' all-seeing pressure
And from their pricked, unsleeping ears.

1841

The Prophet

E'er since the time the Judge on high
Conferred on me a prophet's vision,
I read in ev'ry passing eye
Whole tomes of malice and derision.

When I proclaimed love to the world
And revelation's pure injunction
My kin as one in fury hurled
Sharp stones at me without compunction.

I sprinkled ashes on my head,
In poverty all towns avoided
And live in wastelands here instead,
Like birds, my food by God provided.

The Everlasting Law I keep,
The brute creation is obedient:
The stars hark unto me like sheep,
And play there, joyously and radiant.

Whenever I must make my way
Through noisy towns with hurried paces,
The elders to their children say
With self-possessed, complacent faces:

"Just look there, what do you perceive?
To live among us never deigning,

The proud fool wished us to believe
That God spoke through his lips disdaining."

Mark well, then, children, look at him:
How sad he is, how thin and haggard!
Look well, and see how poor and ragged.
How everyone despises him!

1841

F. I. Tyutchev

{ 1 8 0 3 – 1 8 7 3 }

. . .

As round this earthly globe the oceans pour
All earthly life is wrapped in dreams of wonder;
Then night comes on and with its waves of thunder
    That ocean beats upon its shore.

For thus it speaks: it forces us, demanding . . .
Now quivers by the pier our magic barque;
The tide comes up and bears us from the landing
    And deep into the welt'ring dark.

The vault of heaven with stellar glory rounded,
Mysterious, peers downward from the height—
As we sail on by blazing gulfs surrounded
    Across the wide abyss of night.

1828

There is about these autumn evenings bright
So touching, so mysterious a pleasure:
The eerie tint of trees, now dark, now light,
The languid brush of crimson leaves to treasure,
The misted-over muted azure hue
That hangs above the sorrow-orphaned valleys,
And like forebodings when a storm is due,
A chilling, gusting wind makes fitful sallies;
Decay and near-exhaustion—and on all
That meek and gently smiling evanescence
Which in a thinking creature we would call
A God-bestowed all-suff'ring acquiescence.

1830

Silentium!

No word, keep secret and withhold
Your feelings and your dreams untold—
But in your deepest soul of all
Permit their rising and their fall
Like stars that shine at night, unheard;
Just contemplate them—and no word.

How can the soul itself impart?
How can another read your heart
And comprehend the how and why?
A thought once uttered is a lie;
So leave the crystal springs unstirred;
Be nourished by them—and no word.

Within yourself then learn to live—
The soul that lies within can give
A world of secret magic joys;
They would be drowned by outer noise
By light of day dispersed unheard—
Attend their singing—and no word! . . .

1832

．　　　．　　　．

I love the rite of Luther's congregation,
Their services are solemn, spare, austere,
These simple shrines, these walls completely clear,
I understand their lofty implication.

Do you not see? Prepared for her last passing,
For one last time faith stands before your sight:
She herself has not yet made the crossing
But now her house stands empty for the flight—

She herself has not yet made the crossing,
Behind her she has not yet closed the door . . .
The hour's at hand, has struck . . . Now pray for
    blessing,
You pray here one last time, then nevermore.

1834

My soul is an Elysium of shades,
Of shades all wordless, beauteous, and glowing;
No thought from our tormented time invades,
Of grief and joy they are alike unknowing.

O soul of mine, Elysium of shades,
Small wonder that from life you keep your distance,
As you, the phantoms of that better past that fades,
Shun this unfeeling crowd's existence.

1836

Day and Night

The spirit world we may not see,
That nameless gulf, is shrouded over
And hidden by a golden cover;
Thus do the gods on high decree.
Day—this most splendid shroud is thee,
Day—for us mortals, animation,
The ailing soul's alleviation,
That men and gods delight to see.

But let day fade and night commence;
The blessed veil is torn, revealing
The fateful world it was concealing,
And hurled incontinently hence . . .
The gulf lies naked to the sight
With its black horrors of perdition,
'Twixt them and us lies no partition:
And that is why we fear the night!

1831–39

When locked in murd'rous toils of wants and cares,
When all things pall—and life, a stony burden
Bears down on us—there comes all of a sudden
A breath of joy to catch us unawares.
Remembrance comes to waft round and caress us,
Life's weight now ceases briefly to oppress us.

In autumn, too, it sometimes happens so,
When all the fields are empty, groves denuded,
And skies lie wan o'er sullen vales secluded,
A wind that's warm and softly moist will blow,
A fallen leaf before it skipping, wheeling—
Our spirits feel as if the spring came stealing . . .

1849

Bestow, O Lord, thy gracious pardon
on one who plods with weary feet,
like some poor beggar past a garden
and onward through the summer heat;

who sees, through ornamental railings,
the shade of trees, vales rich in grain,
cool dells denied by iron palings,
a hint of far, light-flooded plain.

'Tis not for him that tree and creeper
entwine in grateful welcome there;
'tis not for him that clouds of vapor
mark fountains, floating in the air.

That azure grotto, misted mountain,
in vain his longing gaze draw now;
a dewy dust steals from the fountain,
but not to cool his burning brow.

Bestow, O Lord, thy gracious pardon
on one who bears his lifetime's load,
like some poor beggar, past a garden,
along a hot and dusty road.

1850

Last Love

Ah, when our last years come in sight,
How sweet, how ominous love's onset . . .
Shine on, shine on, departing light,
As love's last gleaming fades to sunset.

The shadow covers half the sky,
Only westward beams still glisten—
O evening light, why must you fly?
Hold back, oh, stay, enchanting vision!

What though the blood should thinly crawl,
Must then the heart desist from caring?
O thou, the final love of all!
At once pure bliss and pure despairing.

1852–54

Seated there upon the floor,
She picked through each familiar letter,
And like gray ash that glows no more
She took them up and let them scatter.

Then, taking up each page afresh,
So strangely did she look upon them
As souls freed from the cage of flesh
Might then look down on what had borne them . . .

How much of life they held enshrined,
Events beyond recall amassed there!
So many moments brought to mind
Of love and grief, joy and disaster!

I stood in silence by the door,
Prepared to kneel in adoration;
Great sadness moved me to the core
Like some sweet spectral visitation.

1858

．　　　．　　　．

She was oblivious the livelong day;
Her body lay by somber shade surrounded.
The tepid summer rain was almost gay,
The droplets cheerfully resounded.

And slowly she came to herself again
And once again awakened to sensation
And listened long, forgetful of her pain,
Sunk deep in some half-conscious meditation . . .

And then, as if communing with her will,
She spoke at last, her power of speech returning
(I stood close by, quite dead, though living still):
"And still for all of this my heart keeps yearning."

You loved all this, ah yes, no one but you,
Not one till now has had such love to offer!
Oh, God! To think of all I have lived through,
And still my heart remains intact to suffer . . .

1864

Through reason Russia can't be known,
No common yardstick can avail you:
She has a nature all her own—
Have faith in her, all else will fail you.

1866

A. K. Tolstoy

{ 1 8 1 7 – 1 8 7 5 }

．　　　．　　　．

Should you love—be it a furnace
Should you threaten, be in earnest
Should you swear, then make it hot
Should you strike, give all you've got!

Should you argue—speak not coldly
Should you punish—lay on boldly
Should you spare, hold nothing back
Should you feast, let nothing lack!

1850–51

O land of mine where I was bred,
Hoofbeats wildly pounding
Screaming eagles overhead
Wolf calls far resounding!

Hail, O land I hold so dear!
Mighty forests growing!
Midnight birds that thrill the ear,
Clouds, the steppe wind blowing!

1856

. . .

As wave after wave of the turbulent sea
    Rolls in as it roars to exhaustion . . .
My dear, I'm afraid that, in staying with me,
    Naught stands between you and misfortune;
From hope and despair in the highest degree,
From wandering thoughts that approach and then
        flee,
Love's flow and its ebb—in proportion!

1856

The Lord, when arming me for living,
Placed love and anger in my breast,
And raised his strong right hand in giving
Instruction on which path was best;
Breathed mighty words of inspiration,
Imbued my heart with fervent strength;
But temper harsh on his creation
The Lord did not bestow at length.
My wrath I spent on causes needless,
My love knew neither let nor stay,
And blow on blow I suffered, heedless;
In parrying, I faint away.
To face their blizzard's hostile clamor
I ventured out bereft of armor
And perish, wounded in the fray.

1857

You are a victim of life's grief:
You offer it no opposition,
A river-born autumnal leaf,
You drift along in meek submission;

You're like the stubble field's gray smoke:
Whichever way the wind is veering,
It simply spreads out like a cloak,
The cloudward journey ever fearing;

You're like the apple blossom's pride,
When heavy snow has curved it double:
You cannot cast your gloom aside,
And life has bent your back with trouble;

You're like some sunken springtime glade:
When all the world is scent-delighted,
The nearby mountains cast their shade—
And you alone of all are blighted;

And as from melting snow there pours
Into the glade cascading water,
Just so into that heart of yours
The grief flows in from every quarter!

1858

N. A. Nekrasov

{ 1 8 2 1 – 1 8 7 7 }

Farewell

Farewell! Forget our love's declining,
The days of misery and pining,
Forget the storms, forget the tears,
Forget the stings of jealous fears!

But days when love's bright sun was glowing
And tender beams on us bestowing
As gaily stepped we on our way—
Bless and recall them ev'ry day!

1856

from *Reflections by a Main Entrance*

Do you know of just one habitation,
No such corner have I ever known,
Where your farmer and your preservation,
Where the Russian muzhik does not groan?
How he groans on the roads, in the furrows,
How he groans in the prison-yard burrows,
In the mines on a chain gripping tight;
How he groans in the barns for his sorrows,
On the steppe under wagons at night;
How he groans in his own little hovel,
God's own sunlight can't gladden the drudge;
How he groans in town where he must grovel
At the door of some mansion or judge.
Take the Volga: whose groan there goes winging,
Floating over the great Russian stream?
It's a groan that with us is called singing—
As the barge haulers strain in their team.
Volga, Volga! . . . Your springtime excesses
Cannot flood all the fields close at hand,
Like the great grieving lot of our masses
Overflows all the earth in our land—
Where the folk are, they groan—ah, heartrending!
What can *mean* your great groan never-ending?
Will you wake one day bursting with might,
Or, the power of your destiny owning,
Have you done all you could in your plight—

Made a melody much like to moaning
And in spirit relinquished the fight? . . .

1858

from *Frost, the Red-nosed*

No storm, but the forest is drumming,
No mountain becks race to the plains,
The Frosty Commander is coming,
Patrolling his mighty domains.

He looks—has the snowstorm come sweeping
And buried all paths through the trees,
And are there no fissures still peeping,
Can that be bare earth that he sees?

Are the pine tops all feathery frosted,
The oaks with fine pattern adorned?
The ice on the waters thick-crusted
To manacle great lake and pond?

He comes across trees, stepping lightly,
And strides across crackling floes,
The sun as it shines glinting brightly
Across his rough beard as he goes.

For nothing impedes the magician,
Hark! Nearer he comes, grizzled white.
And now he takes up his position,
Above her at dizzying height!

As up to the pine-top he races,
His club through the branches he swings,
And eager to sing his own praises,
A loud boastful ditty he sings.

"Pretty maiden, be bashful no longer,
You see what a Frost Lord am I!
I'll wager no man who was stronger
Or handsomer e'er caught your eye?

"Fogs, snowstorms, or blizzards in motion
The frost can subdue in a trice,
I'll go to the wide-spreading ocean—
And there build a palace of ice.

"One thought and the greatest of rivers
Will vanish deep-laden, and then
Great ice bridges, too, I'll deliver,
Beyond the attainment of men.

"Where waters ran babbling freely,
So recently flowed deep and wide,
Men walk across ice firm and steely,
And caravans cross from each side.

"I love to seek out an interment
And frostily deck out the dead,
And freeze up the blood in its ferment,
And ice up the brains in the head.

"To frighten the thief and the sinner,
To startle the rider and hack,
I love when the evening grows dimmer
To set up a deafening crack.

"Old women will blame it on spirits,
And run home as fast as they can.
But drunkards afoot or in stirrups
Are much better sport for my plan.

"Without chalk I whiten their faces,
And light up their noses like wax,
And freeze their beard fast to their traces,
Try chopping them free with an ax!

"I'm rich, I've no need to count treasure,
My fortune can never decay;
I deck out my realm beyond measure
With diamonds and pearls every day.

"Consent my bright kingdom to enter
And you will be queen of it all!
And reign amid glory in winter,
And not wake in summer at all.

"Come in! I'll give warmth like a lover,
A palace of blue set aside . . . "
And the Frost Lord was waving above her
The great mace he brandished with pride.

"It's warm now?" calls down the enchanter
From pine-top where he lies at ease.
"Oh, yes!" the poor widow makes answer,
Beginning to tremble and freeze.

The Frost Lord came down somewhat lower,
Once more waved his mace in the air
And whispers now tender and slower:
"It's warm now?" "Oh, yes, lover fair!"

She's warm—as her stiff body staggers.
The Frost Lord has touched her at last:
He breathes in her face as he swaggers
And on her fall sharp-pointed daggers
His hoary white whiskers have cast.

And now Frost before her was looming!
"It's warm now?" he murmurs once more.
The form of her husband assuming,
He kissed her as in days of yore.

Darya's lips and her eyes as they glistened
The white-haired enchanter then kissed.
The sweet words to which she had listened
When Proklushka spoke them, he hissed.

So pleasant and restful, half dozing,
To hear all those love words so sweet,
That Darya could feel her eyes closing,
The ax dropping down at her feet.

The poor widow woman is smiling.
It plays on her lips as they drowse,

Her lashes with white down are piling,
And frost needles sit in her brows . . .

No sound as the soul, slowly dying,
To sorrow and passion grows numb.
You stand there and feel the soul sighing,
By silence of death overcome.

No sound, and you see the great forest
A vault of blue sky, sun and tree,
Arrayed in a dull silver hoarfrost
And full of great marvels to see.

Alluring, inscrutable, hidden,
Profound and indifferent . . . But now
An odd sound of rustling unbidden—
A squirrel traverses the bough.

The squirrel caused snow to come sifting
On Darya, while tensing to leap.
But Darya stood stock-still, unshifting,
Enchanted and frozen in sleep . . .

1863

A. A. Fet

{ 1 8 2 0 – 1 8 9 2 }

My dear, mere words have no power—by kisses alone
    one may conquer . . .
  It's true, in your letters to me, it is a great pleasure
    to note
How the ebb and the flow of thought and emotion can
    hinder
  Your hand as it tries to commit either or both to the
    page;
It's true I write verses myself and humbly submit to
    the goddess,
  Many the rhymes I possess, many the meters
    command . . .
But, of all, I love best the rhyming of mutual kisses,
  Tender caesura of lips, free-flowing meter of love.

1842

.　　.　　.

Breathing seems much easier at nighttime,
Somehow more ample . . .
Even the city's less crowded!
Open your window:
Quiet and subtle
The air currents flow by and cool you.
The sky, though! The moon, though!
Ah, that old moon, the magician!
As if all the rooftops
Were covered in mirrorlike glass,
The spires and crosses—all diamonds;
Past the moon, the horizon below
With distance grows brighter, more limpid.
Gazing and breathing,
You hear your own breathing within,
The chime of a far-distant clock,
The cry of the watchman,
The occasional clatter of wheels,
Or the cock-crow that heralds the dawn,
Along with the sunrise comes sleep swooping down
　　　on the eyelids,
Bright as a phantom.
Head starts a-nodding—how sad to be torn
　　　　　　　　　　　　from the window!

1842

The Old Park

The final summer blooms make ready now to fade
And wait dejectedly as frost each flower closes;
The maple's fingered foliage is reddening in the glade,
The sweet pea's day is done and petals rain from roses.

The day has dawned behind a gloomy stand of firs,
But brightness gives the birds no cause for jubilation;
The repetitious, piping bullfinch dulls the ears,
The blue tits' mocking chirp prompts only irritation.

An ancient summerhouse above a cliff is raised.
Two lions without paws extend a staircase greeting
And unknown people's names carved, alien, half-
    erased,
Here intertwine and form an imagery fleeting.

A glance. Beneath my feet, a sheer wall to the plain,
Immobile fir trees stand and draw the eye to follow,
The narrow mountain path cut deeply by the rain,
A twisting yellow snake, runs down into the hollow.

The sun has broken out from cloud-banks and its
    beams
Now pierce the valley shades with sudden lightning
    flashes.
From here I clearly see the lakelet's pulsing streams,
And, moored above the weed, the trout, stock-still and
    plashless.

Alone. No step I hear behind me in the dew.
My heart is filled with gloom, my eyes in fretful
    motion,
While out beyond the pines, a cupola of blue,
There stands the passionless, the pitiless great ocean.

Like gulls' wings in the height, there gleams a
    whitened sail.
I wait for her to sink, but she holds course unveering
And, sliding slowly by along her curving trail,
Like some lost wisp of cloud, melts slowly,
    disappearing.

1853

By the Fireside

In semi-darkness embers glimmer,
Transparent flamelets writhe and twist,
As butterflies on poppies shimmer
Their plashing wings of amethyst.

A brightly colored throng of places
Attract, beguile the weary gaze
And indecipherable faces
Peer out among the ashen grays.

Now rise, harmonious, caressing,
The grief and joy of years, while yet
The soul deceives herself, dismissing
Such pity, such intense regret.

1856

To the Muse

Is it for long you deign to visit my seclusion,
Compelling me to pine beneath love's sovereign sway?
Whose form this time, I pray, embodies your illusion,
Whose tender tones assumed to gain your winning
     way?

Your hand, please. Sit. Ignite your torch of
     inspiration.
Sing, kindly one! All's still; your voice I fully own;
I tremble and begin, in kneeling trepidation,
To memorize the song you sing for me alone.

How sweet to put aside the petty day's vexation,
To blaze up or subside at promptings of pure thought,
And sensing close at hand your mighty visitation,
To ever-pristine words give ear and so be taught.

Then fill, celestial one, my sleepless nights unbroken
With many blissful dreams of glory and of love,
And with that tender name, so softly to be spoken,
On what my mind has wrought grant blessing from
     above.

1857

. . .

Up in the hay one evening, darkling,
With face toward the heavens I lay,
While choirs of stars alive and sparkling
Lay strewn along the Milky Way.

The earth, a fitful dream, insensate,
Receded swiftly out of sight,
And I, of Paradise first inmate,
There face to face beheld the night.

Was I then swept through midnight's chasm,
Or did the star swarm sweep toward me?
It seemed a mighty hand in spasm
Had grasped and held me, dangling free.

With mind in disarray, heart-sickened,
I measured with my eye the fall
Down which with every passing second
I drowned and drowned beyond recall.

1857

The stars glowed red in leaf-still weather
    And it was thus
We two gazed at the stars together
    And they at us.

When all the host of heaven come stealing
    Into the breast,
Cannot the breast withhold, concealing
    Something at least?

All that preserves or prompts life's ferment
    From infancy,
All that is borne off to interment
    In secrecy,

Than stars more pure, than dark more tender,
    Black night more dread,
All this, in eye-to-eye surrender
    Was what we said.

1859

Never

And I awoke. A lidded coffin—fingers
Thrust upward with an effort and I scream
For help. Ah, yet the recollection lingers
Of deathbed throes—but this is not a dream!
Like parting cobwebs, almost without trying
I burst the rotted boards where I was lying

And rose. How sharp it seemed, this winter light
Outside the entrance! All doubt was confounded—
I saw the snow. No door denied my sight.
I set off home. Would they not be astounded?
The park I knew, my footsteps never faltered.
Yet all appeared to me so strangely altered!

I ran through snowdrifts. Deathly trees stood chill,
Their motionless great branches high and airy,
But not a track, no whisper. All was still,
The kingdom of the dead in lands of faerie.
The house at last. A scene of ruination!
My arms dropped to my sides in desolation.

The village slept beneath a shroud of snow,
No path was there on all the land around it.
Yes, there it lies; the little church I know,
The hill, the ancient tower where bells resounded.
Like a pilgrim, snow-girt, climbing high,
It rises clear against the cloudless sky.

No winter birds, no insects spot the snow.
I realized; the earth had long since frozen
And perished thus. To whom, then, did I owe
The breath within me? Wherefore was I chosen
To make this journey? My mind's intuition
Was linked with what? And what was its
    commission?

Where shall I go, where no embrace can be?
Where time combines with space to lose its meaning?
Return then, Death, make haste to gather me,
The fateful burden, living's final gleaning.
And thou, the frozen corpse of earth, fly on
And bear my corpse for aye when I am gone.

1879

To the Muse

You came, were seated. Happy and uplifted,
I now repeat your sweet caressing line,
And if I seem to you but sparely gifted,
No less than others' jealousy is mine.

Your freedom ever zealously protecting,
I kept the uninitiate far hence,
Their servile tumult angrily rejecting,
And any profanation of your sense.

Unchanging thou, in secrecy most hallowed,
Upon a cloud unseen from earth below;
Imperishable goddess, starry-haloed,
With grave and pensive smile upon your brow.

1882

Butterfly

You're right. With feather-light configuration
    I do enthrall.
My velvet self, my living agitation—
    Two wings is all.

Whence my appearance, what my destination?
    Do not inquire.
I choose this fragile flower for my station
    And now—respire.

How long shall I, inactive, resting idly,
    Respiring stay?
One second's space; then, twinkling wings spread
      widely,
    I'll flit away.

1884

BIOGRAPHICAL

NOTES

VASILY ANDREYEVICH ZHUKOVSKY
Born January 29, 1783,*
in the village of Mishinskoye in Tula Province

* This and all dates following refer to the old Russian calendar, which differs by twelve or thirteen days from its modern counterpart.

Illegitimate son of a small landowner and a captive Turkish woman who lived on his estate, Zhukovsky received what was then the equivalent of a university education, though in literary matters he was mostly an autodidact. In his twenties, he made a living as a private tutor and later a magazine editor. In the former capacity, he had the misfortune of falling in love with his, as it were, half-niece; he asked for her hand and was turned down by the girl's mother. This unfulfilled passion became what, in various fashions, fueled his writing for the next three decades. He was relatively unknown until 1812, when he achieved immense popularity with his patriotic "A Bard Among the Russian Warriors," which attracted the notice of the court. A few years later, he assumed the position of reader to Her Majesty and, subsequently, tutor to the heir to the throne. In this capacity, he was able to intercede on behalf of various writers, notably Taras Shevchenko, Alexander Herzen, and Pushkin; also, this appointment enabled him to travel in Europe. At the age of fifty-eight, Zhukovsky went into honorable retirement and married the eighteen-year-old Elizabeth Reitern, daughter of a German painter and Zhukovsky's close friend, and spent the last twelve years of his life in Europe. He died April 12, 1852, in Baden-Baden.

A cross between a sentimentalist and a romantic, Zhukovsky is a highly versatile poet with distinct mystical proclivities. Between romantic individualism and the romantic sublime, he opted for the latter. Zhukovsky's favorite genre was the ballad, which he literally introduced to the language, Russian literature at that juncture being relatively young. He both translated ballads and composed them, but, given the novelty of the form and the emphatic lyricism of his rendition, an attempt to distinguish between translation and original work in Zhukovsky's case is not warranted. Often, in Russian editions, Zhukovsky's translations of foreign authors are printed as his own, without any indication of the source. That's justifiable, since these ballads became an integral part of the corpus of Russian poetry and allowed the Russian language to absorb a considerable amount of Western cultural history, especially medieval lore, for which Russian literature has no counterpart. "A poetic uncle of both German and English devils and witches" (his own words), Zhukovsky translated into Russian the works of Goethe, Schiller, Byron, Thomas Gray, J. H. Herder, J. L. Uhland, Robert Southey, G. A. Bürger, and Sir Walter Scott, as well as Homer's *Odyssey*. "In prose," Zhukovsky once remarked, "the translator is a slave; in poetry, he is a rival."

KONSTANTIN NIKOLAYEVICH BATYUSHKOV
Born May 18, 1787, in the city of Vologda,
some 350 miles east of Saint Petersburg

Descendant of an old aristocratic family, Batyushkov lost his mother at the age of seven and was brought up and educated in private foreign pensions, mostly in Saint Petersburg. At the age of twenty, he entered the military service and took part in various campaigns, notably in the Great Patriotic War of 1812 to 1814, which took him to Germany, France, and, briefly, to England. Upon returning to Russia, he retired from the army and settled in Petersburg, was widely published, and joined the literary society Arzamas. In 1818, he entered the diplomatic service and was sent to his beloved Italy, where, after four years, at the age of thirty-four, he fell prey to a hereditary mental illness, from which he never recovered. He died of typhus thirty-four years later, in seclusion in Vologda, on July 7, 1855.

Though more a classicist than a romantic, Batyushkov qualifies for neither definition because of the peculiar melancholic sobriety of his verse. Its highly mellifluous texture has a tendency to obscure its darker utterances, and it is rather by virtue of his earlier works (inspired by Tibullus, Horace, and Anacreon) than of his maturer period that Batyushkov is regarded as the precursor of the "harmonious school" represented by Pushkin's Pleiad. A later Batyushkov is the master of an extended elegy that covers in its progress much cultural, historical, and psychological ground, with a somber, often ecclesiastically toned coda. He also wrote a number of influential essays about literature and the visual arts and translated Tibullus, Torquato Tasso, Evariste Désiré de Parny, and segments of Dante's *Commedia*.

PRINCE PETER ANDREYEVICH
VYAZEMSKY
Born July 12, 1792, in Moscow

Prince Vyazemsky belonged to one of Russian nobility's most ancient families, which traced its line to the first princes of the Kievan Rus'. Privately but excellently educated, he joined the People's Volunteer Corps in 1812 (two horses are said to have been killed from under him in the battle of Borodino). After the war, while in the diplomatic service, he developed views critical of the government; in 1820, took part in petitioning the Tsar to abolish serfdom and in preparing a constitution. Dismissed in 1821, he lived for nine years as a private citizen at his family estate of Ostafyevo, near Moscow, but in 1830 he returned to service and spent the next twenty-five years at the Ministry of Finance, later as head of the Imperial Credit

Bank. Subsequently, he became a deputy to the Minister of Education and in this capacity supervised the Department of Censorship. A reformist rather than a revolutionary even in his youth, in the second half of his long life Vyazemsky came around to a pro-government position and was regarded by contemporary literary opinion as a reactionary. Having lost most of his family and having outlived his closest friends (notably, Pushkin and Baratynsky), in these years Vyazemsky frequently traveled in Europe and the Holy Land: after 1863, he resided mostly abroad and died in Baden-Baden, on November 10, 1878.

A superb yet underestimated poet, Vyazemsky is habitually dubbed a classicist—presumably because of his penchant for Alexandrian verse and his clarity of content. A better designation might be "critical realist," if only due to the satirico-didactic tone and character of most of his poetry. Many of them plain narratives or epistles, his poems describe, inform, argue, suggest rather than sing; the effect is more often cumulative than instantaneous. A typical Vyazemsky poem strives to make some point, and in its progress absorbs a great deal of diverse material and pitch. The net result is a sense of unresolved lyricism or, rather, of huge lyrical residue: the lines add up to more than the content aspires to. His politics as much as his aesthetics propel Vyazemsky's verse toward the vernacular; he not only was the closest friend Pushkin ever had but was, in this sense, Pushkin's forerunner. Vyazemsky, however, is the kind of poet who will put an idea in a poem before harmony, who will sacrifice music and balance to the intricacy or accuracy of the thought. He admitted this preference too often for anyone to cite it among his shortcomings. Besides, nothing different could be expected from somebody who, orphaned at nine, had Nikolai Karamzin, the author of *The History of the Russian State*, for his guardian. Topical and hilariously, almost distractingly witty (as in "The Russian God," which Alexander Herzen translated into German for Karl Marx, in whose archives it survived), the poems of Vyazemsky's later period offer a rapidly darkening view of a world with which the author has less and less in common; Vyazemsky is extremely interesting to read because he never lies. He also produced a substantial body of absolutely splendid literary criticism. Of still greater consequence, especially for those interested in the period, are his Notebooks, with their mixture of anecdotes, aphorisms, sketches of political figures, contemporary gossip, and literary matters; here Vyazemsky is our Chamfort and La Rochefoucauld in one.

ALEKSANDR SERGEYEVICH PUSHKIN
Born May 26, 1799, in Moscow

On his father's side, Pushkin cited six centuries of Russian nobility; on his mother's, he was the grandson of a black chieftain from Ethiopia (some maintain, an Ethiopian Jew), who entered the Russian Imperial employ under Peter the Great, and whose son earned an officer's commission and, with it, a nobleman's rank. Perfectly bilingual (at home, Pushkin spoke and, allegedly, wrote poems in French), Pushkin at the age of twelve entered the Lyceum, where he received the best education available in Russia at the time and read widely in contemporary French literature and the Latin classics. Also while at the Lyceum—located some fifteen miles from Saint Petersburg, in Tsarskoye Selo—he began to write poetry in Russian and published his first poem when he was fifteen. At his graduation, Pushkin was singled out by Gavrila Romanovich Derzhavin, the most honored poet of the preceding generation; this was a symbolic moment in the history of Russian literature in which the baton, as it were, passed from one epoch and one style to another.

Upon graduating from the Lyceum, Pushkin was nominally

employed by the state department of foreign affairs and settled in Petersburg, where—his talent recognized early—he led a life typical of a writer and a scion of the impoverished nobility. The popularity of his poetry grew as rapidly as his output; so did the attention paid him by the police and the court itself. He was banished from Saint Petersburg to the southern provinces of the Empire in 1821 and spent three years traveling with relative freedom in the Crimea, the Caucasus, and Moldavia, residing in Kishinev and Odessa. This was followed by two years confined to the family estate near Pskov, in the village of Mikhailovskoye. In 1826, when it became clear that he was not implicated in the Decembrist conspiracy, Pushkin was allowed to return to Saint Petersburg and was received by the Tsar, with whom he had a long and frank conversation, in the course of which the Tsar offered to be Pushkin's personal censor, permitting him to live anywhere in the Empire.

For the next eleven years—that is, for the rest of his life—Pushkin remained mostly in Petersburg, with prolonged stays in Moscow, Mikhailovskoye, and family estates. In 1829, he traveled briefly to the Caucasus and, in 1833, as part of his research into the Pugachev uprising, to the region between the Ural Mountains and the Volga. His immense popularity with the reading public did not insure him against attacks from various literary cliques, nor did it offer financial security, which was often threatened by card debts and the needs of his relatives. Also, his fortunes were influenced by the rather unstable attitude of the court toward him and his work, which never displayed a predictable pattern. In 1831, Pushkin married a young Moscow beauty, Natalia Goncharova, who bore him five children. Six years later, hounded by malicious rumors purporting to besmirch his and his wife's reputation, he challenged one of the instigators to a duel and was killed.

There was nothing of greater consequence to Russian literature and the Russian language than this thirty-seven-year-long life. Pushkin gave the Russian nation its literary tongue and thereby its sensibility. With him, Russian poetry speaks for the first time in an idiom that is truly native, in the vernacular. As a poet, he evolved with an extraordinary rapidity, as though nature knew that his time was limited. He writes in all genres and in great quantity; his forte is a short lyric or its opposite, a lengthy narrative poem full of digressions. Influenced since childhood by French writers (among whom, he especially worshipped Voltaire), Pushkin in his early twenties mastered English so as to read Byron and, shortly afterward, to immerse himself in Shakespeare. It is to these two influences that we owe the existence of *Eugene Onegin* and *Boris Godunov*. His verse displays a disquieting, indeed incomprehensible ability to combine a light touch with breathtaking profundity; it never ceases to yield, on rereading, depth after depth, at every stage of one's life; his rhymes and meters reveal every word's stereoscopic nature. As much if not more than in foreign literatures (Pushkin translated from Latin, Greek, Italian, French, German, and English, among others), he was engrossed in Russian folklore and Russian history. The latter gradually began to overshadow poetry, in the form of either historical novel or pure study. His collected works run to eleven volumes, not counting his letters. One-third of this output is prose (criticism, essays, travel, polemic, novels, short stories, and historical works). It is doubtful that toward the end of his life Pushkin coveted a career as a fiction writer; it is true, however, that the greatest literary influence of his life was the author of *The History of the Russian State*, and history is the mother of prose.

Born February 19, 1800, in the village of Mara, near Tambov

One of seven children of a retired army general, Baratynsky lost his father early and was brought up by his mother. In 1812, at the age of twelve, he was sent to the military college in Saint Petersburg, from which he was expelled four years later on charges of petty theft. This episode was no doubt of traumatic consequence not only for Baratynsky's psychological makeup but also—given the family's financial circumstances—for his social standing: Baratynsky then had to enter the army as a private and serve for six years before earning an officer's commission and regaining his nobleman's status, in 1825. While in Saint Petersburg, where his batallion was stationed, Baratynsky befriended members of Pushkin's literary circle and began to publish. He continued to publish in Saint Petersburg periodicals and maintained close ties with his friends when later his unit was transferred north, to what was then Finland; though it is barely a hundred miles from the capital, the poet regarded this as exile. A year after becoming an officer, he retired from the army, married, and settled in Moscow. Marriage provided Baratynsky with financial security, and most of his remaining years he alternated between Moscow and the family estate, occasionally visiting Saint Petersburg. He was published frequently and produced three collections of work, as well as a body of criticism and a short novel. In 1843 he traveled to France and Italy, where, in Naples, on June 29, 1844, he suddenly died. His remains were brought by sea to Saint Petersburg and he was buried in the Alexander Nevsky Monastery.

Though more narrow in scope than Pushkin, Baratynsky is fully his peer and often seems superior to his great contemporary in the genre of the philosophical poem. Pushkin himself remarked of him: "Baratynsky is unique among us, for he thinks."

Thought is indeed the hallmark of Baratynsky's verse; he is the most analytical lyric poet Russia has had. The texture of his lines is the strongest evidence for the "felt thought" thesis, as his argument evolves euphonically and tonally rather than in a linear fashion. Hence the argument's fast pace and its air of implacability. Within a cultural tradition whose main tenor is consolation, Baratynsky is an oddity. Even in his earliest elegies (for which he earned accolades from virtually every corner of the literary community), he is never personal or autobiographical, and leans toward an integrating remark, toward a psychological truth. His poems are denouements, summaries, postscripts to actual or intellectual dramas that have already taken place, rather than a record of them; they are more often evaluations of a plight than its account. Anaphora is his favorite device, and the elasticity of his verse is remarkable. A Baratynsky poem pursues its subject with an almost Calvinistic fervor, and often its subject, indeed, is an imperfect soul that the author fashions after his own. It is to his "psychological miniatures" that the Russian novel of the second half of the nineteenth century owes most, though it appears to have failed to inherit his lyrical hero's stoic, clear-eyed posture. On the whole, Baratynsky's is the most lucid verse written in Russian in that century; that is why, to this day, nearly every poetic school in the twentieth has put him on the banner.

NIKOLAI MIKHAILOVICH YAZYKOV
Born March 4, 1803, near the city of Simbirsk,
to a well-to-do family of the gentry

A perpetual student, Yazykov attended a number of schools, including the Mining College, the College of Road Engineers, and Derpt (currently Tartu) University, earning no degree at any of them. It was while at Derpt, where from 1822 to 1829 he studied philosophy, that Yazykov took to composing poems and drinking songs that quickly became popular among the student body (of which he was an acknowledged leader) and in Saint Petersburg literary circles. After leaving Derpt in 1829, he settled in Moscow, occasionally traveling to Europe for reasons of health (the consequences of the intemperance of his youth), until his death on December 26, 1846.

Chiefly known as the "bard of grape and merrymaking" (as he often billed himself), Yazykov in fact represents a far more complex phenomenon. He is perhaps the only true romantic among the Pushkin Pleiad; rationality is the last thing to make its presence felt in his lines. Although he never states his beliefs or political convictions, the sheer exuberance of his early work led his young liberal-minded upper-class readers to regard Yazykov as one of their spokesmen. This contributed to his reputation initially and detracted from it eventually when, repentent and soul-searching, Yazykov took to voicing orthodox, Slavophile views, which echoed, rather distinctly, official attitudes. For all that, Yazykov's is the most ringing, most vigorous verse of the period, similar to but sometimes besting Pushkin's. The precision of his vocabulary, often enriched with his own neologisms, and the buoyancy of his rhythms, together with the vividness of his imagery, leave an impression of tremendous energy harnessed by meter. He did perhaps more than anybody else to liberate the poetic idiom of the time from its stylistic constraints, to invigorate the diction and heighten the pitch. Nikolai Gogol once remarked about Yazykov that he had lived up to his name, for *yazyk* in Russian means "tongue."

MIKHAIL YUREVICH LERMONTOV
Born October 3, 1814, in Moscow,
to a family of impoverished nobility

Having lost his mother at a tender age, Lermontov was brought up by his rich grandmother, since his father, a retired infantry captain, was of limited means. At the age of thirteen, he enrolled at the Moscow University preparatory college and, after two years there, entered the university. In 1832, Lermontov abandoned his studies, moved to Saint Petersburg, and entered the Cavalry and Guards Officers Academy, graduating from it in 1834 and joining the Imperial Hussars Battalion stationed in Tsarskoye Selo. The next three years saw him more often in Saint Petersburg salons than in the barracks; it is also the time of his first appearance in print. In 1837, upon learning of Pushkin's death in a duel, he wrote an impassioned poem, full of grief and anger, in which he all but charged court circles with the assassination of the poet. This reflected the public's view of the duel, and the poem enjoyed wide circulation. When it ended up at the palace, Lermontov was arrested and dispatched to the Caucasus for combat duty against local tribes. When allowed to return to Saint Petersburg a year later, he resumed his social and literary rounds while nominally reassigned to his Hussars' detachment in Tsarskoye. His reputation in literary circles (he's often regarded as Pushkin's heir) and in polite society was by then quite high—although he is openly sardonic and skeptical of both; he was writing and publishing in great quantities. In 1840, Lermontov challenged the son of the French ambassador to a duel, with the result that the military court ordered him—allegedly on Nicholas I's direct instruction—back to the Caucasus. In 1841, having distinguished himself in action and been decorated, he returned briefly to Saint Petersburg, hoping for an honorable discharge, but after a few weeks in the capital was ordered to leave again in forty-eight hours for the Caucasus. Three months later, on July 15, 1841, in Pyatigorsk, Lermontov was killed in a duel with a fellow officer. As in the case of Pushkin, the public saw Lermontov's death as assassination by proxy.

Obviously autobiographical, Lermontov's poetry is that of a

man apart, not only in any given social context, but in the world as such. This posture, which is in itself the first cry of the "superfluous people" theme that came to dominate the Russian novel later in the century, could be defined as romantic, were it not for Lermontov's thoroughly corrosive, bilious self-knowledge. Seldom in practice and almost never on paper does Lermontov strive to square his ideals with reality; indeed, he all but revels in their disparity. Such tendencies, given Lermontov's life, of course allowed the public to perceive him as the period's bard of discontent, of protest, of moral opposition to the system. Lermontov's diapason, however, is wider: his feverishly burning lines are aimed at world order itself. A poet of immense lyric intensity, Lermontov is at his best when on the attack or in his rare moments of serenity. His verse, normally leaning toward tetrameters, came to him in an almost effortless surge, which accounts for his proclivity for a lengthy poem that, regardless of the content, nearly always has an air of confession. Though he worked in various genres, he particularly excels in his battle pieces (one of these, "Borodino," was the germ that grew, according to Tolstoy, into *War and Peace*), which draw on his firsthand experience of the military. Of three things to which this poet of negation repeatedly pledges allegiance—war, the motherland, and freedom—only the first has emotional or literal content for him; the other two are to him metaphysical categories rather than sentimental or political realities. The uniform he wore wasn't a disguise: he was a fighter in more ways than one, the main enemy being his own psyche. Lermontov brought to Russian literature a far more complex sensibility than did his contemporaries or predecessors: the characters in his novel *A Hero of Our Times* (much admired by Chekhov) are heroes of our times as well.

Born November 23, 1803, in Orel Province

Tyutchev came from an old gentry family. He received his elementary education at home and at the age of fifteen enrolled at Moscow University. Shortly after graduating in 1822, he went into the diplomatic service and was sent with the Russian mission to Bavaria, with the rank of undersecretary, in which position he served for the next fifteen years. While in Munich, he befriended Heinrich Heine, whom he subsequently translated, and Friedrich Wilhelm von Schelling, whose nature-philosophy can be seen to have influenced Tyutchev's writing of this period. In 1826, he married a young widow, Eleanor Peterson, née Countess Bothmer, though, by all surviving accounts, Tyutchev appears ill-suited for any enterprise entailing personal responsibility. In 1837, as a result of his scandalous affair with yet another young widow, Baroness Ernestine Dörnberg, née Pfeffel, Tyutchev was transferred to the Russian mission in Turin, with the rank of senior secretary. A year later, his first wife died, and in 1839 he received the Foreign Ministry's permission to marry Baroness Dörnberg. He was chargé d'affaires pro tem, and abandoned his duties to go to Switzerland for a honeymoon, in the course of which he lost secret codes and other important papers. This led to his dismissal from the diplomatic service, and he returned to Munich, where he resided with his family (by now he had five children) until 1844, writing—in French— a number of essays on international politics. In 1844, one of his political essays caught the eye of the Russian monarch, who found its content congenial to his views, and Tyutchev, after twenty-two years of living abroad, returned to Russia, where he was reinstated into the foreign service and began to work for the Foreign Censorship Committee in Saint Petersburg (he was in charge of foreign printed matter subject to permission or ban in Russia), eventually becoming its chairman. At the age of forty-seven, he fell in love with the twenty-four-year-old Elena Denisieva. This affair, which lasted fourteen years and caused great consternation in official circles, gave Russian literature a body of extraordinary poems, the immortal "Denisieva Cycle." With the death of its heroine in 1864, Tyutchev fell in love once again, with her friend, a forty-five-year-old widow, E. K. Bogdanova, née Baroness Uslar. This last passion left no trace in Tyutchev's verses but colored the remaining years of his life, in the course of which Tyutchev traveled a number of times, for reasons of health, to Nice, Geneva, and Carlsbad. He died on July 15, 1873, in Tsarskoye Selo.

Considering the length of Tyutchev's life, the corpus of his poetry is relatively small: about four hundred poems. He was first noticed for his publications in 1836 in two consecutive issues of *Sovremennik* (*The Contemporary*), edited by Pushkin; but as he was absent from the literary scene, this publication was of little consequence for his reputation. It was only after his return to Russia, toward the end of the 1840s and the beginning of the 1850s, that his work came to receive full recognition. Tyutchev emerged as the most significant and atypical voice of the first half of the century. A distant relation of Baratynsky, Tyutchev, too, worked in the vein of philosophical poetry, except that his verse shows a greater appetite for the infinite than for the particular. As a rule, a concrete detail in his poem seldom serves as a springboard for cosmic perspective; it is rather the other way around. His poems are usually short, compact, and arranged according to a detectable thesis-antithesis-synthesis principle. Thematically, his output falls roughly into three categories: meditations on nature, love lyrics, and civic poetry (i.e., poems about current politico-historical matters). Of the three, the latter are the least palatable; neither before nor since has the Russian autocracy had a more loyal bard.

Tyutchev's political views are highly orthodox, and even his infrequent criticism of the throne is criticism from the right. He was a strong adherent of Pan-Slavism; perturbed by the volatile political situation in Europe, he often fervently urged—both in his poems and in his essays—the civilized nations of the West toward a closer alliance with conservative Russia. Though translating his civil servant's rigid political philosophy into verse, Tyutchev displays—especially in his later love poetry—a tendency toward distinctly impressionistic patterns, which infuse his keen philosophical insights with a natural, half-haphazard air that makes them memorable and lasting. Of the nineteenth-century Russian poets, he is perhaps the most modern both in his overall posture and in his techniques. Among his ardent admirers were Ivan Turgenev, Fyodor Dostoevsky, and Leo Tolstoy; later, he also found an unlikely champion in Lenin.

ALEKSEI KONSTANTINOVICH TOLSTOY
Born August 24, 1817, in Saint Petersburg

The only son of Count K. P. Tolstoy and a renowned beauty, A. A. Perovskaya, young Tolstoy was educated at home and traveled abroad, in Germany and Italy. He began to compose verse rather early and was encouraged by his mother and his uncle, a professional fiction writer. At the age of seventeen, he was given a junior position in the Foreign Ministry Archive—a traditional sinecure for aristocratic offspring. From 1837 to 1840, he served with the Russian mission in Germany, but displayed little enthusiasm in performing his duties. On the whole, his career in the Imperial administration (where he, given his origins, had remarkable opportunities for advancement) was noted more for vacations than for accomplishments, and in 1861 Tolstoy finally retired from the Imperial service. By this time, he was already well established as a writer of short stories, adaptations of folk epics, ballads, satires, and lyrical poems; also, he had co-authored, with two of his cousins, a concoction of largely absurdist prose and poetry that came to be known as "The Works of Kozma Prutkov." Free of his administrative obligations, Tolstoy concentrated on his literary work, especially on his verse-drama cycle about the Era of Turmoil—the time in Russian history marked by the rule of Ivan the Terrible and Boris Godunov. Of the three plays that constitute the cycle, two were banned from the stage, but the first one, *The Death of Ivan the Terrible*, brought him fame. His novel *The Silver Prince*, dealing with the same historical period, also enjoyed great popularity. Although his lyric poetry was the least interesting part of his oeuvre, nearly seventy poems of his have been set to music by various Russian composers. During the last ten years of his life, Tolstoy, though constantly working, spent more and more time abroad, seeking a cure for recurring migraines. He died on September 28, 1875, at his family estate of Krasnyi Rog, in Chernigov Province, from an overdose of morphine.

Tolstoy is a poet of unique facility and versatility; he is also a superb humorist. The unpredictable and witty texture of his verse, often verging on hilarity, arrests the reader's attention in Tolstoy's poems no less, and perhaps more immediately, than does the story line. The latter, however, is also often absorbing—especially in his narrative historical poems and ballads—due to Tolstoy's very specific historical perspective. Somewhat romantically, perhaps, Tolstoy considers the Kievan Rus' and the Novgorod Republic the golden age of Russian history. He regards the unification of the separate Russian princehoods under the Moscow monarch (necessary to resist the Tartar occupation) as a tragically regressive event that engendered the Tsar's unlimited autocratic power and the state's subsequent bureaucratic apparatus. Or, as Tolstoy puts it in one of his poems, "In opposing the Khan, you [the Tsar] became the Khan yourself." This view is not without merit. Naturally, it set Tolstoy apart from both liberal-minded and conservative elements in the literary establishment, from revolutionary demo-crats, whom he ridiculed, and from Slavophiles, with whom he temporarily sided in the 1850s. Given the record of the country in the century that followed his death, however, what seemed to his contemporaries to be escapist or nostalgic musings has ac-quired the quality of cautionary and largely prophetic tales.

NIKOLAI ALEKSEYEVICH NEKRASOV
Born November 28, 1821, in Podolsk Province

The son of a retired army officer, Nekrasov grew up on the family estate, where he received his early education. At the age of eleven he entered Yaroslavl Gymnasium, which he left in 1837 without completing the course. At the insistence of his father, he was sent to Saint Petersburg when he was sixteen for military training; instead, he attended Saint Petersburg University as an auditor. Enraged, Nekrasov's father cut off all support, and for the next few years Nekrasov led the life of the city poor. He began to compose for the stage, and several of his vaudeville skits met with a degree of success. In the early 1840s, he befriended the influential literary critic Vissarion Belinsky, who arranged an editorial job for him at the magazine *Sovremennik* (*The Contemporary*). By 1847, Nekrasov had be-come its co-owner, as well as the lover of his rather witless partner's wife. In the editor's seat, Nekrasov found himself in his element, and for the next fourteen years the magazine evolved as an increasingly vocal mouthpiece for progressive populist propaganda advocating the abolition of serfdom and defending peasant rights—all but directly calling for revolu-tionary changes. Apart from that, Nekrasov the editor should be credited with discovering Fyodor Dostoevsky (whose "Poor

People" he ran in *The Contemporary*) as well as publishing Turgenev, Goncharov, Saltykov-Shchedrin, Ostrovsky, Herzen, and Tolstoy, among others. The Peasant Reform came to pass in 1861, and in 1866, in the aftermath of a failed assassination attempt on the Tsar, the magazine was banned. Nekrasov, having published a successful collection of poems ten years earlier, was by this time a well-established poet, much revered by the progressive intelligentsia (a class that emerged about this time in Russia, in the wake of the demise of the aristocratic culture). This sentiment, steadily fueled by Nekrasov's epic output depicting the horrible predicament of Russian peasantry, was to outlast his inner circle's grumblings about Nekrasov's reprehensible romantic and gambling habits: apparently, company likes misery more than vice, for the contrast between what he preached in his verse and the luxury in which he dwelt was truly astonishing. In 1868, Nekrasov became the editor of yet another literary journal, *Otechestvennye zapiski* (*National Diary*), which he directed until his death from cancer nine years later, on December 27, 1877, in Saint Petersburg.

Predominantly dactylic and anapestic, Nekrasov's poems are predictably long-winded: his principal genre is the narrative poem. Given the subject matter, his predilection for dactyls (which endow verse with an air of lamentation) is particularly lucky. His diction gravitates toward the vernacular, and the only influence which is detectable in his work is that of folklore. Often, very much in the folkloric tradition, Nekrasov's imagery, consciously realistic and down-to-earth, strays toward surrealistic morbidity. Negligible as a lyric poet, Nekrasov nevertheless suffused his socially concerned lines with a high-pitched lyricism that, combined with compassion and the hopelessness of the subject matter, produces a devastating effect on the reader. A typical Nekrasov poem is essentially a rusticated polyphonic version of a ballad, but with the emphasis not so much on the story line as on detail, on description. A man of keen eye and sensitive ear, Nekrasov is a poet not of revelation but of recognition.

AFANASY AFANASIEVICH FET
Born in 1820, the exact date unknown, in the village of Novoselki in Orel Province

The illegitimate son of a German woman, Charlotte Elisabetha Foeth, Fet was illegally adopted by her Russian husband, Afanasy Shenshin, a retired army officer and landowner. The future poet was brought up and educated on the estate, bearing the name of his alleged father, until he was fourteen, when the illegality of his adoption (as well as of the marriage itself) suddenly came to light. With that, young Shenshin lost both his gentry status and his Russian citizenship and had to assume his mother's surname. The next three years he spent at a German boarding school in what is today the city of Viru in Estonia. In 1838, allowed to return to Russia proper, Fet moved to Moscow, attending Moscow University, from which he graduated in 1844. While at the university, Fet published his first collection of poems, which went largely unnoticed. In 1845, in order to attain gentry status, Fet, who, legally speaking, was a foreigner, entered military service with the rank of private. For approximately thirteen years—first with Imperial cuirassiers in Russia's south, then with uhlans stationed near Saint Petersburg—he pursued his goal of obtaining an officer's commission, necessary to qualify for gentry status. In 1850, Fet published a second collection of poems, which won him high praise throughout polite society, and he became a fixture in the pages of Nekrasov's *Contemporary*. Also, his regiment's proximity to Saint Petersburg helped him to develop personal ties with a number of men of letters, notably Turgenev, Nekrasov, and Leo Tolstoy. In 1857, Fet married a sister of the prominent critic V. P.

Botkin. The next year—the military rank required for gentrification constantly changing—Fet retired from the army and left Saint Petersburg and its literary scene for his native Orel Province, where he had bought land. In the course of the next decade, Fet proved himself a capable landowner and became rather wealthy. When he was fifty-three, an Imperial decree reinstated him as a member of the Shenshin family, with the right to use that surname: his goal was attained.

More absorbed at this stage in agriculture than in literature, Shenshin-Fet poured all his energies into managing the estate, served as his county's Justice of the Peace, and regularly contributed to *Russkyi vestnik* (*The Russian Herald*) on the subjects of farming, property regulations, horsebreeding, etc. In the public discourse on peasant reform raging at that time, he took an understandably conservative position, which badly affected his literary reputation and earned him the label of serfdom backer. The less strident among his friends accused him of general insensitivity toward the ethical choices of the time, or, on the basis of Fet's frequent manifestations of his extreme, idiosyncratic individualism, mused about the state of his mental health. By 1881, Fet had distanced himself from the affairs of his estate and returned to poetry, producing, in the course of the last ten years of his life, four collections of poems as well as a quantity of translations, including, among others, the work of Horace, Ovid, Juvenal, Propertius, Vergil, Goethe (*Faust* in its entirety), Heine, Schiller, and Schopenhauer's *The World As Will and Representation*. He died on November 21, 1892, in Moscow—of self-inflicted wounds after attempting suicide, according to some sources; of a heart attack, according to others.

Fet is a lyrical poet of the highest acumen. The body of his poetry constitutes a collection of what Goethe called "stopped moments"—of arrested states and isolated sensations. The tenor of his art is mostly joyful and celebratory, but even at his unhappiest, Fet concentrates on the emotion itself to the total exclusion of any social or historical context. This gives his poems their extemporal, "Japanese" air. He sings not of a beautiful woman but of the beauty in a woman, "not things themselves, but ideas about things." His verse is fluid and supple, and both nature and inanimate objects emerge from under his pen with palpable reality. His poems very often have the character of diary entries, of verbal snapshots, with an entire life seemingly condensed into one "day," one instant. Fet is exceptionally good at depicting fleeting, transitional states of the human psyche; hence his high standing with many a writer of psychological novels, especially Leo Tolstoy. A conscious aesthete and determinist in the fashion of Schopenhauer, Fet sought to rid his verse of any shred of didacticism, and constantly laid emphasis on sound and tune over meaning. Many of his poems were set to music and became popular love songs; the greatest partisan Fet had in his lifetime was Tchaikovsky.

J.B.